CW01647526

The True Hero's Journey

in Fairy Tales and Stone Circles

Best wishes,

Andrea

Andrea Hofman

The True Hero's Journey
in Fairy Tales and Stone Circles
Andrea Hofman
Ting Press

Published by Ting Press, Switzerland

Editor: Beth Hammock

Cover and Interior design: Davis Creative, DavisCreative.com

ISBN: 978-3-033-06973-2

1. SOC011000 SOCIAL SCIENCE / Folklore & Mythology
2. SEL032000 SELF-HELP / Spiritual
3. SOC002010 SOCIAL SCIENCE / Anthropology / Cultural & Social

To my beloved heroines,
my daughters Felicia and Elea

Table of Contents

Author's Note

Throughout this book, I will use the terms "folk tale" and "fairy tale" interchangeably.

To make reading easier, I decided to mostly use the female form "heroine" or to stay general with the word "protagonist" and "they" as a singular pronoun. It also serves to differentiate the more "feminine" heroes in fairy tales from the male hero stereotypes in classical myths. So, unless I further specify it, the talk is always of both genders.

The terms "Sun", "Moon", and "Earth" are capitalized to emphasize their planetary nature, which will become more apparent in Part II of this book.

All folk tales which are not presented in full length here can be found on my website www.andreahofman.com.

Introduction

"If you want to change the world, change the way you look at things, and the things you look at will change."

Gandhi

I was sitting in the warm café at the Stonehenge Visitor Center reflecting on the connection between fairy tales and the old stone circle here. The stones are no longer standing and holes are all that remain. The holes are called Aubrey holes. *Once upon a time* fifty-six bluestone pillars stood here in a large circle. They shimmered in a mystical blue hue and fulfilled their sacred purpose to track the cycles of the Moon and the Sun, as well as their points of intersection, the lunar nodes. It was one huge balanced soli-lunar calendar, which equally integrated the cycles of the Moon with those of the Sun, considering that there were thirteen lunar months within one solar year. The Aubrey Circle was built to observe the dance of these two main luminaries up in the sky, which create life on Earth. Independent of any weather conditions, this stony calendar was able to reveal the position of the Sun and the Moon against the stars, indicate their relationship to one another, precisely show the lunar phase and the state of the tides, and accurately predict lunar and solar eclipses.

Once upon a time is also how a fairy tale begins. The stories coax out of their listeners a faint memory of a long-lost world inhabited by peculiar folks, fantastic beings, fairies, witches, dragons, princesses and princes, and heroes. It was the world of the Neolithic builders, who invented the tales to remind people of the old matriarchal values and to demonstrate how the balanced Sun-Moon calendar worked.

Fairy tales mostly present a world where all struggles result in justice and benevolence. Here, things change for the better and wrongs get turned into rights. They promise a story which will eventually lead to a happy ending. If not, it is quite clear why not. Their world is straightforward: the good ones win and the bad ones get punished. But the reason why some of them are also called "tall tales" is because we think their stories are lies, impossible and a little crazy. Still, we are inspired by their wisdom and use their symbols and figures as archetypes to learn more about ourselves. But what if the fairy tales contained a truth that was even more directly applicable? What if the folk tales were to instruct us on *how* our lives should truly be when balanced? Are they holding a message, just as the German word for fairy tales "Märchen" implies? "Mär" means "message" and the end term "chen" is belittling it. Is here a message which got belittled?

For over a decade, I was searching for this message and found not only one, but two messages that were hidden in folk tales. One of them was conveying the old matriarchal ways of living in sync with Mother Nature and the other was the balanced soli-lunar calendar. Both survived to this day due to the tales' oral passing on by the illiterate folk who were so close to nature that they understood the tales' talk about the inter-connectedness of all beings. Over the millenniums, they must have always spoken directly to the heart of the hardworking illiterate folk, who got up with the first rays of the Sun, but still sensed the mystical qualities of the Moon push and pull like tidal waves through their veins. The tales spoke about visible and invisible things, of this world and the other, of secrets in nature and the between-and-betwixt times and places, where the two worlds met. These were things the folk knew about, it was part of life like eating and sleeping. The tales were therefore conveying how life worked in the cosmic order.

The fairy tales are our very European wisdom stories, as it turns out. However, such tales were potentially dangerous for the patriarchal world, and that's why they got belittled. The messages speak of matriarchal values of collaboration and mutual care, where there are no gender and status differences. Such values of equality were indeed not suitable for patriarchal ambitions.

The calendrical know-how of the long-forgotten Aubrey Circle here at Stonehenge was well-hidden in the structural build-up of the *wonder tales*, a subgroup of the fairy tales. Tucked away in an entertaining story of protagonists on their journey through an adventure, there was a teaching of utmost importance, the teaching of *the true hero's journey.*

Common people and storytellers alike who passed on the tales sensed that they also contained an instruction, which provided them with a map to help navigate life on this beautiful and mysterious planet called Earth. Whenever the path got lost and divine intervention was needed, it could be re-found by heeding the tales' advice. The alignment with the cosmic order could always be found again, if the calendrical rhythm in the hero's journey was sensed and the lunar energy included.

What is the *True* Hero's Journey?

The *true* hero's journey is the story of any human being who walks her path of life on planet Earth. It is true for several reasons. For one, it is attuned to the cosmic cycles. The wonder tales, which contain a complete form of the hero's journey, unlike the monomyth[1], show a calendrical alignment to the cosmic cycles of the Sun and the Moon. They demonstrate the profound solar and lunar influence on a person's life and destiny. If we want to become aware of the forces that shape us and the world around us, we need to become conscious of the cycles of these two main lights up in the sky. Therefore, the wonder tales and their heroic journey illustrate how our reality gets subtly "woven" by their cycles. It is the process that goes on behind the veil of creation.

The word "Mär" on a closer look implies that the fairy tales hold *"a piece of news or a message of something, an event or a truth, which is well-known or deserves to be well-known, so that it merits to be spread."*[2] The creators of the wonder tales knew that who wanted a peaceful and abundant life needed to be aware of the creational soli-lunar cycles. So, this would be quite a truth worth spreading, wouldn't it?

Another reason it is called the true hero's journey is because it is a much older version of the monomyth and is based on insights primarily gained from oral mythology. It uses protagonists to exemplify real-life people in real-life situations on their path through real life. Yet, the reason why these tales feel like mere products of fantasy to us is because we

---

1 The "monomyth" or the "hero's journey" is a sequence of adventures a mostly male hero in a story goes through. Ideally, along the road he will change into a wise person, as he has certain insights. It can be found in myths from all over the world. See also "The Hero with a Thousand Faces" by Joseph Campbell, Abacus, 1975

2 "Die Märchen der Brüder Grimm, eine Einführung" (The Tales of the Brothers Grimm, an Introduction), Heinz Rölleke, Reclam, 2004 (translated by the author)

do not understand how they were meant to be understood any longer. We think they are untrue, made-up stories since we no longer look at life through the lens of the Neolithic elders, who created the tales. When to us an encounter with an animal in the woods is nothing special, a fairy tale protagonist might view it as an encounter with a spirit helper. If we were looking at things from that perspective, we might judge what happens to us differently. So, understanding how the hero's journey can be talking of true life asks of us a change of perspective. We need to better understand the fairy tales and their worldview.

The Sun got favored over the Moon

During my journey of discovery, which I am sharing with you in Part I and II of this book, I came to learn that the evolution of imbalance, where humanity changed from matriarchal values to patriarchal, was partly brought on by humans living by an unbalanced calendar. After the Aubrey calendar was forgotten and the bluestones were used for other purposes, people started to live by another time measurement. It favored the Sun over the Moon, disregarding the fact that both are creative forces on equal terms, shaping all that grows and flourishes on Earth. Favoring only the Sun brought forth in history a whole new set of values and myths celebrating masculine solar heroes only and disregarding all feminine and lunar qualities. Over time, the lunar attributes got suppressed, demonized, or belittled, just like the fairy tales.

This has had far-reaching consequences and caused a vast imbalance in people's personal and collective lives, as five millenniums of patriarchal history has proven. While the cosmic cycles kept turning their endless rounds, humans' awareness changed.

We could even say that the cycles don't care how we look at them; whether we are aware of how they shape our personal lives doesn't matter to them. However, when looking at the wonder tales and taking them as instruction, we notice that there is a higher instance that does care a great deal. The tales speak of support by spirit guides with mysterious and helpful qualities, guiding the protagonist to a deeper connection with nature and the divine. It is a fascinating world, which seems to be at the disposal of anyone who is seriously interested in finding her way back to the natural rhythms.

Obviously, we have forgotten how blissful life can be if we collaborate with spirit, nature, and all beings around us. We are all part of the divine creative energies and the cosmic cycles that shape our lives. As over time the lunar energy went missing in societies, the wonder tales served to urgently appeal to the conscious and unconscious layers of human awareness to go retrieve it.

Even though the Moon energy was misinterpreted as a demonic, adversary force and feared as evil, the heroine learns on her journey that it is not the lunar energies she needs to fear, but rather the humans who suppress and demonize them. Over the past patriarchal millenniums, a *web of lies* has been created, where a vicious cycle of trauma and compensation has taken its course. Victims and perpetrators started to alternate their roles, each traumatized to the core of their hearts. It seems to be the scope of fairy tales to heal these wounds. The wonder tales, to be more specific, with their true hero's journey are the ones that point the way back to an alignment with the divine cosmic order. The quest of the heroine therefore serves to recover the missing lunar energy and move first herself, then her environment, and, finally, her entire society into alignment with the natural cosmic order. Only then will a society be capable of peace, balance, healthy renewal, and abundance. When this alignment is reached, the community will create a *web of dreams* together, a reality where benevolence and collaboration prevail, and individuals can unfold freely according to their potentials.

A Timeless Truth

Astrology proved to be the key to unlocking the at least five-thousand-year-old message in the wonder tales, revealing their connection to stone circles such as the former Aubrey calendar. These are the teachings of the Neolithic astronomers, who were our European ancestors and wisdom-keepers. Their truth is timeless and universal, the teachings still applicable today. Just like the protagonists in the wonder tales, we can detect our individual heroic journeys, our own path of life, by looking at the solar-lunar cycles, or to be more precise, at the north lunar node, which is their point of intersection. We can start to finally make sense of our biographical twists and turns, since, as it turns out, we are all on a hero's journey at every moment in our lives. This insight will lead to a heightened appreciation for ourselves, as well as a deeper trust in the invisible creative forces behind life. Then, we get to experience how a life in-tune with the destiny- shaping forces automatically leads to more serenity, joy and balance, just like modeled in the wonder tales.

I conducted numerous personal interviews and studied biographies and compared them to wonder tales and found the true hero's journey really is the story of any human being who ever walked the path of life on the face of the Earth. Our developmental journey from birth to death illustrates how our potential to evolve from a normal person into a wise elder gets triggered by the ever-changing cosmic influence of the Sun and the Moon.

If you want to take a peak and see where you are currently located on your hero's journey, skip to the tables in Appendix A, look up the segment and the degree of your age, and turn to the corresponding segment chapter in Part III of this book. Then return here for a journey of discovery through Part I and II.

I have overcome a great deal of fear to stand firmly in these findings that clearly do not align with conventional thinking patterns. Yet, I think this material is way too interesting and thought-provoking to not be shared.

The years from my first notion that there *should* be a match between the hero's journey and the astrological chart, to the moment of finding it was my personal quest. I had to transform my take on life from being a modern-thinking human, conditioned to be disconnected from the natural laws, to getting in-tune again with the creative forces, which shape our world and destiny. I had to question and let go of patriarchal belief systems, which I had never dared to question before. I had to grow from a conformist into a discerning person who dared to say no and follow my own train of thoughts. It was a long process for an obedient middle-class daughter to come to this place, where I now share my quite revolutionary findings with you here.

I hope this different way of viewing life and the world around you appeals to you and will serve you personally as much as it serves me, my family, friends, clients, and the many test persons and interview partners I shared it with. You will adopt a new perspective on your life, once you become aware of the cycles that shape it. Or, as an interview partner put it: "I can suddenly feel the cosmic order; it gives me goosebumps." You will see how inner and outer events are connected. They begin to make sense in a broader context. And if you apply the skills of folk tale heroines and heroes you can follow your heart and live up to your soul's higher purpose. This again will make you feel balanced and serene.

Part I

Matriarchal Wisdom

The First Message in European Fairy Tales

Chapter 1

A Mechanism to Happiness

"So, first you must find in yourself that which moves you."
Joseph Campbell

There was a time in my life, when I started to see social ills everywhere around me. It seemed to me that life was all about manipulative games and dependencies. I was in my late thirties and had just given birth to our second daughter. I felt I should not be as dependent as I was. For example, I wondered, "Why, as a family with small children in Switzerland, were we not supported better?" Having children was looked at more like a burden on taxpayers than at what it was, a contribution to the renewal of society. In general, there seemed to be an attitude that, "If you want babies, it's your own responsibility to bring them up." Out of this reason, a growing number of our friends decided to not have children at all. Having children could bring you to the verge of poverty in no time and should the marriage not hold, you'd become a poor single parent, even in a country as wealthy as ours. There was a mentality of wanting to be where the grass was always greener, and in Switzerland, that surely was where the money was.

As a society, we were forgetting that should all of us decide to stop having children because of financial interests, there would eventually come a time where there would be no next generation. And what, then, would all the old people do with their stacks of money? They might end up lonely and greedy, no one at their sides to share their joys and sorrows with. I could suddenly get enraged about issues I had never thought about before, even though we were in no trouble—yet. With the birth of our second child, however, I realized that in my world, having children came with a price.

The price was dependency, because money comes with strings attached. A heap of debts, from the bank, the car dealer, the tax bureau, and the parents was secretly growing. I soon would have to learn that I could not be the independent person I wanted to be and, at the same time, indebt myself for participation in "the good life." Without noticing, I was maneuvering myself onto the wrong side of life, I was no longer on the side with the greener grass.

A Quantum Moment

In this time of growing tension, out of nowhere, I had a *quantum moment*[3], which triggered a change in my life that suddenly let me see a doorway, where there was none before. I had just put down my ten-month-old daughter for her midday nap and made myself comfortable on the sofa with a steaming cup of tea. It was the only time during the

3 The term *quantum moment* is inspired by William R. Miller and Janet C'de Baca's book "Quantum Change, when Epiphanies and Sudden Insights Transform Ordinary Lives," The Guilford Press, 2001

day I had to myself, as my older daughter had just left for afternoon school and there was no client counseling session scheduled for the afternoon. At that time, it was still common for children in Switzerland to come home for lunch, which made it especially difficult for mothers to work outside of the house. I was looking out at the blooming apple trees in the garden and it wasn't long until I put down my cup and dozed off a bit.

Suddenly, in this state between dream and reality, a thought jolted through me like lightning. It made me sit up and grab pen and paper. Entering my mind out of the blue was a sudden flash of inspiration, accompanied by an incredible burst of energy. I had never experienced something in this way. Well, instantly, I knew I wanted to be—ta-da—*a screenwriter!*

Now, where did that come from? I had to write it down since it was not in alignment at all with any occupation I had at the time. I was working part-time as a social worker for refugees and doing astrological counseling. Yet the weird thing was, though it made perfect sense to me in that moment, it was only when I excitedly called my husband to tell him the good news that I realized by his reaction that it really did not make much sense at all. I wasn't a writer, nor did I have anything to do with film. Ok, I had lived in Los Angeles for a while as a student taking theater classes at the local community college, but that was long ago, and I had always preferred the theater and not film.

Yes, I admit that I dreamed sometimes, like so many, of being a bestselling author, writing novels on the porch of a little lake cabin and my husband serving me tea. He knew of this fantasy of mine, but still he then burst out laughing when I called him and told him of my flash of inspiration to be a screenwriter. "Ah, I know what this is," he chuckled, "you are entering midlife." Well, yes, I soon would turn 40, but not until over a year later. I now burst out laughing, too, and had to admit that it all did not make that much sense, since I wasn't even writing regularly. I usually spent the nap times of our baby preparing my astrology counseling sessions. I was still only dreaming of writing. The idea of screenwriting seemed, on second thought, totally out of context with anything in my life. My husband continued to tease me, and I continued to try to sell my new idea to him.

I felt such a jolt of energy when the inspiration hit as if a fire was instantly lit inside of me. It was as if a door had suddenly presented itself to me, and all I needed to do was step through to reach an enticing, visionary land where I could reinvent myself. Now, this needn't exactly be *screenwriting*, but that thought sure bestowed me with the necessary enthusiasm to go explore something that was in no context to my life whatsoever. I guess, it gave me the freedom of mind I needed so badly to envision a way out of my growing dependencies. If I did not change anything, my life would continue its laid-out tracks down a road I did not want to go. It would lead me further and further away from the bliss I had once known.

Times of Bliss

A few years before this moment of inspiration, I had an amazing, life-changing six-month road trip through the United States with my husband and our five-year-old daughter. It was a dream come true to take time off from daily life and plunge right into the spectacular

American wilderness. We started out in sunny California in springtime and it wasn't long until we realized that the further off the beaten path we traveled, we were not only happier, but also more attuned to nature. Depending on the location, we had very different animal encounters. One place was full of little frogs, while at another campground, we encountered wild geese, deer, raccoons, praying mantises, owls, snakes, beavers, and coyotes. We began to perceive all wildness around us as ensouled, and a deep connection started to develop. An absolute highlight was watching a tarantula fiercely defending her territory. Once, I saw a spotted owl looking straight at me, then in the blink of an eye, it flew off in silence. Was this real? It was as if I had an encounter with a mysterious otherworldly being.

It became evident that there was always one kind of animal encounter that was dominant in one place. Did this have a meaning, were they in communication with us? Soon we found precious books such as "Spirit Animals" by Victoria Covell or "Animal-Wise" by Ted Andrews that described the deeper meaning behind animal sightings, and it became clear that the animals were corresponding to our state of mind. We started to reflect on ourselves and began to greet the animals. A kind of exchange set in, and with it, a reverence for what was happening. Then we began to greet the places we stayed overnight and thank them upon leaving. It felt right to do this, since we were intruding in that space.

At a campground in Arizona, we met a lady who said she could see fairies. She showed us how to burn pine resin on a piece of charcoal, something which supposedly pleased the fairies and would help us to see them. This friendly lady even gave us a little pan to burn the resin, which was shaped like a kettle you might see in fairy tales. That night, I meditated with so much pine smoke that I got a bad case of diarrhea, but over time, as we said goodbye to the friendly lady and moved on, I found myself a method to move into the spirit world beyond, where I found many an inspiring guidance along the way.

It was amazing. I would sit in a meditative state before what I learned was *holy smoke,* and I'd close my eyes. Then, a flat line appeared before my inner eye, and in my imagination, I was invited to view the line as a curtain, lift it up and slip underneath through. On the other side, a whole other world opened: a vast landscape only slightly lit in a dusky glow surrounded by rocks. Usually I encountered a friendly council sitting around a fire, and I could ask them anything I wanted.

Over the following years, when meditating I often retreated to this place of sanctity. Here I felt unconditional acceptance and benevolence. Here I could come back to a state of serenity when I had lost it. Sometimes, I would just sit with them, at other times, we were dancing in a circle and at other times, when I felt especially sad and imbalanced, I was asked to lay down on a large, flat rock and they did a healing ceremony on me. To my own surprise, these kinds of meditations helped me sort out many issues and always brought me back to my center.

I was still not able to see the fairies like the friendly lady we had encountered in Arizona, but I seemed to have gained access to an inner world, which at the same time was the invisible side of life, where inner guides, maybe ancestors, were caring about what happened in my physical world. In my mind's eye, they looked like native elders who emanated wisdom and benevolence, but I could not identify them more closely. From then on, I felt connected to the spirit of the land all around us, wherever I was, on our trip and back home. A sensation of deep connection to the creative source—without and within—developed during that trip, resulting in feeling safe and sound like a baby in Mother Nature's arms. It was such a sweet feeling, as if I was held close to her heartbeat and nothing bad could ever happen to me, to us. It was sheer *bliss*.

From what I know now, this feeling of bliss must have come from tuning into the energies of nature and from our nomadic way of life with the camper, which allowed us to move *whenever* we liked to *wherever* we felt drawn to. It let us find our own rhythm. Due to that freedom and our growing communication with everything around us, we seem to have attuned ourselves to something far deeper, the cosmic cycles in nature.

After we got home and back in our daily routines, that feeling of bliss started to fade, though we tried hard to regain it. Slowly but surely it deteriorated and all that remained was the longing for it—and the knowledge that something was missing in our everyday life. In addition, my two part-time jobs let me witness the daily struggles of others, as well. Life often couldn't be further from bliss for them. While we recently had been on a freely chosen adventure with all our possessions fit into a van for six months, I now met refugees who arrived in our country with nothing but what they could carry during their flight. They certainly did not call it an adventure. On the contrary, they were highly stressed and traumatized. On top of everything, they were now exposed to a rather egotistical society where those in need seemed to be a nuisance, because they cost too much money without producing anything of value.

In such a system there was not much room for compassion, acceptance and appreciation. Values seemed to rate people, men were more valuable than women, fathers more than mothers, sons more than daughters, adults more than children, the rich more than the poor, the old more than the young. It seemed wrong to me that our society was not placing children first, children who were a society's future. Suddenly, I perceived hierarchies everywhere around me. But weren't we all just humans with an innate desire to be loved and appreciated for who we were? Didn't we all have the right to a blissful life? All seemed oriented toward a mentality of "Look after Number One," celebrating idols who live as if there is no tomorrow and buying into a concept of "Let the devil take the hindmost." However, as we experienced on our trip, bliss was not coming from buying things at the shopping mall, rather it came from balance, harmony, and freedom out in nature.

The Returning of Light

The more I questioned the systems and hierarchies of Western society, the more I evoked adversaries in my life. A gap opened between those who agreed with me and those who wanted me to stay quiet and not shake things up. My role asked me to be a perfect mother, caretaker at home and on the job, to remain an obedient daughter, employee, patient, and tenant. I certainly was not allowed to question those with status and power. On the contrary, if I diligently did what I was asked and re-invested my money into the products that were targeted at my age group, I was a well-adjusted citizen. You know, that alone should have made me happy, because next to the refugees' heart-wrenching fate, mine certainly looked pretty good. And it *was* pretty good, what could I complain?

Still, I saw my clearly carved out role everywhere. I was assigned to it in childhood—the friendly woman who always said yes, who should work harder, pay more taxes, and higher rent, while at the same time increasing consumption and debt to do so. I saw the financial gap opening wider, because I should also be of assistance to the older generation, while not losing sight of my children's well-being. One day, I realized that I was caught in a trap. My willingness to do things that I felt were right, my willingness to be a good citizen, and to be of service and to care was being taken advantage of all the while my own happiness was decreasing. One evening around Christmas it all crashed over me. Where had my bliss gone? I wrote in my diary: "I am desperate. Where is my bliss? Is there a mechanism to happiness? If such a thing were to be found in astrology it certainly could help me and my clients."

I clung to that question, as if it were my returning light at the winter solstice. It gave me hope to go looking for such a mechanism, if not for me, then for others. At that time, the first books on happiness were coming out. I read them all—next to researching how a good screenplay could be written.

The following summer, our family, now complete with a second daughter and a dog, drove up to Scandinavia, where we re-found a little bit of the long-lost bliss in Sweden's untouched nature and its residents' forward-thinking mentality. We spent our vacation there, far up in the north, where moose cross the streets and wolves roam the woods. While I was meditating on a rock near a lonely lake, I had some deep insights concerning the astrological aspect circle, which years later proved to be the missing link between the hero's journey and the astrological chart. But at that moment in Sweden, I knew nothing of the hero's journey yet.

This was soon to change when some months later, I came across Joseph Campbell's work. After my quantum moment, instead of getting my pencil sharpened and jotting down my ideas for a screenplay, as any aspiring writer should do, I sat down at the computer and delved into research on screenwriting. To me this was only logical, because not having much time and racing toward my fortieth birthday, I needed to get this right from the beginning.

The first thing I came across was something called "The Hero's Journey" and it absolutely matched my no-fuss attitude: there existed a template that almost guaranteed a successful play, you only had to write your story according to that structure. Movies like the ones in Star Wars trilogy were following this archetypal structure, also called "the monomyth." My curiosity was awakened, and in order to be even better equipped to write my future blockbuster, I read Joseph Campbell's book "The Hero with a Thousand Faces," where everything was thoroughly explained.

According to the book, a hero would depart from his regular life, following a call from destiny, or he would refuse that call and stay home, which would not be a good choice. If he did leave for the journey, though, he would meet many difficulties along his path, which he had to master, but he would eventually be transformed and return with an elixir, having become a whole and wise person. Now that sounded like the mechanism to happiness, I was looking for.

The hero works himself through these different stages:

1. The call to adventure
2. Commitment or refusal of the call
3. Supernatural aid

4. Crossing the threshold
5. Road of trials
6. Apotheosis
7. The ultimate boon/elixir
8. Return or refusal of return
9. The magic flight
10. Rescue from without
11. The crossing of the return threshold
12. Master of two worlds and the freedom to live

Was this *hero's journey* my way to re-find bliss? I certainly saw myself confirmed by one of Campbell's other books called "Pathways to Bliss, Mythology and Personal Transformation."

So, my focus shifted away from screenwriting to wanting to tie the structure of the hero's journey to the astrological chart. I committed to this task with all my heart, reading up on the great heroic quests in literature, such as "Odysseus" or "Hercules," trying to understand their journey and connect it with a planetary action. If that is not calling for major planetary action when somebody breaks out from regular life, what is?

Campbell referred to Schopenhauer, who suggested that by looking back on life, a plot could be made out. The idea that life was one long story appealed to me. This would also mean that we could kind of write out our own life. Or was there even a script to our life? Was there such a thing as a mapped-out process by planets, which served like a blueprint for our journey, a blueprint on how to transform life for the better? If there was, it most definitely *had to be visible* in a person's astrological chart.

Innumerable baby naptimes later, instead of writing my screenplay, I did what was closest to my heart: researching the answers to those essential questions. If the monomyth was such an archetypal theme, it would be easy to discover it in my chart, and then I could quickly move on to writing. So, I thought. I would only need to answer some questions, like

- How do I know if I am on a hero's journey?
- If I am, where am I at?
- How and when does change occur?
- What is the gain?

Once I knew the answers to these questions, I felt certain I would be all set. I researched all the material about myths and the monomyth that I could find. Then I tested it out with innumerable astrological techniques, connecting planets, asteroids, trans-Neptunian objects, midpoints, Arabian points, Sabian symbols, you name it, with various aspects using harmonics and dials. But the years went by and nothing fell into place to make a story whole. The pieces remained scattered. To be honest, the mythological stories felt scattered to me. It felt as though the gods and goddesses of myth, the protagonists in classical mythology and their equivalents in astrology, were all but huge individualists. I got lost in their complexities and I got lost in the complexities of astrology. No consistent story line, no hero's journey in the stars, only random puzzle pieces here and there, scattered together.

In the meantime, my movie script was still not being written. I didn't mind because I was so absorbed with this frantic search for a "mechanism to happiness" in myth and astrology that all potential blockbusters of mine just had to wait. The quantum moment might have not wanted to make me a screenwriter. Who knows? Rather it intended to send me down the track of discovering the hero's journey's connection to the cosmos. It was going to take me a decade until I could finally solve that riddle and another three years to understand what it actually implied and write this book.

Chapter 2

A Treasure Chest Full of Tales

"If you want your children to be intelligent, read them fairy tales. If you want them to be more intelligent, read them more fairy tales."

Albert Einstein

Slowly but surely, I changed from the analytical world of astrology into the fascinating world of stories. I found myself using story motives everywhere—in counseling, in the classes I taught, and at home, where I was reading "Harry Potter" to my older daughter and fairy tales to my younger one. I could see why some say storytelling is a human instinct. The brain thinks in stories, researchers say.[4] Whatever we as humans encounter, feel, and learn, we want to communicate. When we pack an experience into a story it connects us to our group, which again makes us feel safe and like we belong. The storytelling instinct of our human species cannot really be stopped, researchers say, nor can it be curbed. Experience and wisdom need to be shared and passed on. The conveying of experiences like, "Behind this little wood

4 "Der Erzählinstinkt—Warum das Gehirn in Geschichten denkt" (The Instinct of Narration—Why the Brain Thinks in Stories), Werner Siefer, Hanser Verlag, 2015

there is a lake, but watch your step, the shore is slippery," could therefore well be as old as humanity, they say.

I learned that with our stories we contribute to the common perception of the world we live in and thus help create a shared outlook of this life on Earth. Ultimately, which stories we tell defines the culture of our tribe. Not only that, it shapes what we perceive and what we ignore, what we think is okay, and what we look at as threatening. The more the dos and don'ts are reassured by stories, the more they get established as values, and future stories will have to go along those lines to be accepted by the listeners. In prehistoric times, long before writing was invented, the stories of a community were held sacred. The elders knew about the power of a narrative and they knew how important it was to tell *the right kind of story*. For if it wasn't in alignment with the natural laws and rhythms, it would mess up people's perceptions and cause *a web of lies*, as we will see in Chapter 4. People would lose sight of how they were connected and embedded in nature and would start to be alienated from their own source.

I became aware that the invention of writing must have opened a whole new way of conveying an idea in history. From then on, anybody who was able to read and write could share it with readers and thus could shape their outlook on life. The power of a narrative suddenly was distributed into many hands, its shared content fixated in the zeitgeist of its recording. One needed neither to be an elder nor a priest to impart wisdom, any insight could be shared, whether universally valid or nonsense. Over time, the stories no longer served the purpose of conveying wisdom on overarching issues, like natural laws, but rather they could be used as a personal take on life, mirroring individual experiences and fantasy, with the risk of promoting ideas that would not serve to maintain harmony and balance in a community.

The Elixir

At one point in his journey, the hero finds the boon, also called the *elixir*. According to Campbell, it usually was found or received when the goal of the quest has been achieved. Then, the elixir needed only to be carried back into everyday life, something which could be another long or a short story.

A shift of focus brought me my elixir.[5] In an unforgettable moment, fireworks of recognition were ignited in my heart. I suddenly received access to a vast chest of solutions—a chest full of fairy tales.

It was one of those early fall evenings, when the last rays of sun paint everything in golden light. A remnant of summer's warmth was in the air, yet the ground was already damp, and the chestnuts had already started to fall. Children were eagerly picking them up, turning to their mothers with triumphant smiles. That night, I was not bending down for chestnuts myself, because I was out for a ladies' night without my children. It was a bit peculiar though, since my friend and I were to go to a storytelling event. She took me there because she knew my interest in stories. We walked up the stairs to the community hall and inside, we noticed in the subdued lighting of exotic lanterns and candles, a

5 In the *true* hero's journey, I found the elixir to be showing up as something soothing, life-sustaining, which appears twice in a slightly different form. It is a gift that provides the protagonist with new hope and appears when she has learned to listen to her inner, spiritual guidance and act accordingly. Therefore, the elixir always shows up at the right time and in the right place to tend to her wounds and give an implication, to where the path leads next.

fanciful, rich buffet with delicacies from what seemed the lands of the folk tale's origin. Excitement was in the air and soon got a hold of me, too. We encountered a group of highly motivated ladies, students who had just finished a school for storytellers specialized in maintaining the intangible cultural heritage of telling folk and fairy tales.[6]

They told us that in contrast to Oriental storytelling and storytelling in native tribes, in Europe the telling of tales had disappeared from the public, from markets, and streets about 500 years ago. This was the time when the witch trials started to pick up full swing, making it dangerous to publicly spread anything but Biblical content. At the same time, the invention of book printing also changed people's needs for stories. Who was educated would read works of literature and philosophy, next to the Bible. The oral story tradition on the other hand remained among the poor, illiterate people. Up until recently, the folk tales were told mostly in the countryside and for entertainment purposes. In remote areas all over Europe, the folk tales were still told in special gatherings, especially during wintertime, to make long evenings shorter, while spinning or doing other kind of mending work. People would meet in barns or in each other's kitchens after a long day's work to listen to stories.

A scene of Astrid Lindgren's book "Emil in Lonneberga" came to my mind. The famous Swedish author of children's books such as "Pippi

---

6 The United Nations Educational, Scientific and Cultural Organization (UNESCO) safeguards orally transmitted folklore as a folk's intangible cultural heritage. Its website states: "Cultural heritage does not end at monuments and collections of objects. It also includes traditions or living expressions inherited from our ancestors and passed on to our descendants, such as oral traditions, performing arts, social practices, rituals, festive events, knowledge and practices concerning nature and the universe or the knowledge and skills to produce traditional crafts." See ich.unesco.org/

Longstocking" was inspired by tales heard in such a setting. During her childhood in rural Sweden in the early 1900s, she herself had heard her first fairy tale in a kitchen when she was a young girl. This allegedly awakened her lifelong passion for storytelling. In that scene, Emil's whole family is gathered on a dark November afternoon around the kitchen stove. While the mother, the old maid, and the daughter are combing wool and spinning, the father and his farmhand do mending and repair-work. Underneath the table, the children play with the cat. When Emil's little sister pretends she is a wolf, the old maid starts telling stories about the hungry wolves roaming the dark winter woods of Sweden. It doesn't take long before the children are begging for more, and the old maid becomes a storyteller. The scene is written so vividly that one has the feeling of sitting in the kitchen with all of them.[7]

Now, it was time for my friend and I to take our seats and enjoy the stories the storytelling graduates would tell us. At first, I was just curious, then, with every tale, my heart opened wider and wider, until tears of joy and remembrance filled my eyes. Was this possible? Not only did I feel like a little girl again, to whom fairy tales were being told in a precious, cozy moment, I journeyed with the heroines from their initial suffering to the well-deserved happy ending. There I was with them, in the dark woods, lonely and afraid, then courageously moving on, because there was no other way but to move ahead. As the storytellers described the encounters with helpful dwarfs and cruel witches, I rejoiced and suffered right alongside them. Oh, I hoped they would

---

7 In The Land of Legends, the museum of oral storytelling in Ljungby, Sweden, you can find much on the folklore that inspired Astrid Lindgren. These were the tales of her youth. Besides, the museum vividly portrays the old worldview in folk tales. See sagobygden.se/en/the-land-of-legends

make it home safe and sound, but then again, I knew there was a good chance, because in fairy tales, they mostly would. All of this is somehow made possible under the wing of a well-meaning power, even if that power is not always visible.

When the storytellers made their bow before the break, I was so happy to finally release all my pent-up emotions into frantic applause.

According to neurologist Dr. Gerhard Hüther, when a fairy tale is told from memory, more so than when it is read, something important happens in the brain of the listener. The safety of a storytelling setting activates the emotional centers and substances are produced which promote the building of new connections between nerve cells. The folk tales promote the enhancement of compassion, as well as the abilities to form better relationships, to overcome obstacles, and to give hope. No wonder I felt so enthusiastic. When things get dark and dangerous in the tale, but are told in a cozy storytelling setting, there can be a learning effect of a new "virtual" situation. However, it is of the utmost importance that the darkness and the danger are followed by a happy ending. The resolution then ensures the listener, who has started to identify with the story, that the actions were not meaningless after all. Therefore, Hüther claims storytelling of "Märchen" to be the highest form of teaching, since the suspense and the action of the tale are felt yet are not happening in reality.[8]

8 "Weshalb Kinder Märchen brauchen – Neurobiologische Argumente für den Erhalt einer Märchenerzählkultur" (Why Children Need Fairy Tales—Neurobiological Arguments for the Preservation of a Fairytale Narrative Culture), Gerald Hüther, University of Göttingen. gerald-huether.de/populaer/veroeffentlichungen-von-gerald-huether/texte/maerchen-gerald-huether/

I knew right then and there, I had found something very precious to me. My body was flushed with all these brain chemicals, making me happy and wistful and reminiscent all at once, and at the same time, I knew that this was the kind of story I had been looking for all along. It felt as good as when I was sitting in "my world beyond" in meditation surrounded by benevolence and serenity. I knew nothing at the time of the mysterious message hidden in fairy tales, but I sure could feel it.

After the break, where the audience got to taste some of the delicacies related to the tales, one of the storytellers told this Jewish parable, which put into words what I was sensing.

The Truth and the Folk Tale ("Märchen")

Truth was walking down the streets all naked, as on the day of her birth. Nobody wanted to invite her into their home, on the contrary, everybody who met Truth ran away in fear. One day, just as Truth was again walking through the streets, deep in thought, sad and bitter, she encountered Märchen. Märchen was wearing colorful and splendid clothes, which filled every eye and every heart who met him with delight.

Märchen asked Truth: "Tell me, dear friend, why do you look so sad?"

"I am in despair. I am old and all alone, nobody wants to know me," answered Truth.

"Well, it is not because you are old that people do not like you," Märchen replied. "I, too, am old, but the older I get, the more people love me. Let me share my secret with you. People love when one is disguised a bit,

embellished in decorative fabrics. Let me lend you such clothing, as I am wearing it, and you will see, people will love you, too. "

Truth heeded Märchen's advice and now embellished herself with the clothes of Märchen. Since that day, Truth and Märchen walk together.

Later that evening, I felt more serene and relaxed than I had in ages. This sensation strongly resembled the long-lost state of bliss, the bliss of being in sync with the universe. I felt so rich, for I had been presented with a treasure chest full of tales, which had the capacity of restoring bliss for me. I had come home to the fairy tales of my childhood and I knew instantly this must be the elixir, *my personal elixir*, Campbell was talking about. In the world of fairy tales, mutual caring prevailed, with no telling the other he was wrong and that he needed to go clear up his own inner mess, like I was being told a lot lately. To the contrary, things could be changed, and obedient women succeeded in moving out of their dependent daughter roles. In the end, all was different, and justice prevailed.

These were the kind of stories I wanted to explore. Yes, this was what I wanted to do, I knew it. I, too, wanted to become a storyteller and bring back the memories of magic and healing to people. People who, like me, were longing for bliss, but did not know how to access it. The key had been here, all along, in the form of my childhood tales.

Looking back, I did not know at that moment, that this was an important piece of the puzzle for finding what I was looking for, a mechanism to happiness, the hero's journey as it matches the cosmic cycles.

Becoming a Storyteller

My passion for oral tales was sparked by the storytelling event and its tremendous effect on me. I needed to find out more about those tales and wanted to know how to tell them well. So, over the following years I went to "fairy tale school," and it wasn't long before I turned into an ambassador of folk tales and storytelling.

As I recognized the tales' capacity to soothe me, I wanted to present them to other people. Soon, I was telling tales to all the children I had access to via my younger daughter, whose age group had just started to be interested in fairy tales. I went to birthday parties, nearby kindergartens, schools, and libraries. Oral storytelling had so many beneficial effects, I could observe a similar impact on my audience. Often, I heard back from astonished teachers and parents about how otherwise inattentive or nervous kids were able to follow even long tales.

The regulative impact not only comes from stories that lead up to a good ending, but also from the connection between the storyteller and his audience. The term "by heart" in English is the same as in French "par coeur," and implies that there is a connection between the ear and the heart. The brain transforms what is heard into physical reactions and feelings, as mentioned above. Oral storytelling, therefore, is a way of connecting the ear to the heart and making it more like the sharing of an experience. Also, mystery traditions around the world consider the heart as a gateway into the realms beyond this world, to where the deepest wisdom can be found.

One time I remember about thirty kids sitting on the floor in front of me, and one boy was laying on his stomach, constantly changing position. I had the impression that he hated to have to be there, confined in this room, having to listen to something as silly as fairy tales. I carried on trying to ignore his grunting and rolling from side-to-side. Toward the end of the tale, where the disenchantment finally takes place, he sat up and looked at me with big eyes, bursting out with a sigh of relief: "Ah, finally! I knew all would be fine."

Later he came up to me with some astonishingly insightful comments about the tale. He had been listening so attentively that I must admit, I was pretty taken aback. However, I could relate to him, since whenever I was exposed to folk tales being told by heart, at first, I was restless, then toward the end of a story, a deep relaxation set in and my trust in life was restored.

Soon, I expanded to tell stories also to adults at cultural events, weddings, anniversaries, retirement homes, and even at business events. They seemed to especially like local folk tales, romantic tales, Oriental wisdom tales, indigenous creation stories, or trickster tales. I was glad to rely on the old transmitted folk tales, which were proven by a long tradition of storytelling, to share wisdom without having to proclaim it to everyone.

Chapter 3

Summoning up an Ally

"How are you going to change the situation unless you break the rules?"
Joseph Campbell

Working with my voice when telling stories let me to shed my old skin. I learned that the throat was directly connected to the heart, as I was still working on becoming independent. No longer did I want to serve as a puppet in people's small and large-scale schemes. No longer was I willing to jump on the whim of everybody else's needs and wants, only to end up with empty hands and an empty bank account. Learning the fairy tales by heart opened a gateway to my heartfelt inner wisdom and gave me guidance in how to better deal with these issues. However, the more I refused to play along with societal expectations, the more I was alienated and verbally attacked. How strange that suddenly, the landlord raised our rent, despite the house falling apart, and the bank and our parents increased their claims as well? How paradoxical a situation where, despite the adversity, I was still so happy with my newfound elixir. But still, just as an elixir should do, the tales offered me a safe haven and helped me overcome the difficulties. They were inviting me to mentally withdraw into their realm, while at the same time giving me instructions on how to face the lurking shadows of life. In the tales, at least the shadows could be named, faced, and dissolved. There, doing the right thing leads to just results.

In the meantime, on the outside, it felt as though fairness and collaboration were values only to be found in fairy tales. Every situation seemed to shout at me: "Life is a constant battle and the stronger ones win. If you want a piece of the cake, you must either be submissive or fight. The sooner you accept this, the better it will be for you."

Was this so? Were they right? There seemed to be a sunny side of life, with lots of money, high status, and power. There certainly would be room for me there, but I had to meet certain societal expectations. All I had to do was to give in, fulfill my role, and stop being so stubborn. Better yet, if I backed down and considered all of this as my own inner mess and the shadows I was facing merely my own shadows, I would readily be helped. "Honey, do you need a good shrink? I can give you a name," people told me. "Try this pill, it will help you." The shadows would vanish temporarily, I knew, but they only would go into hiding, that I knew, as well. And I would have sold my soul.

I was way too stubborn and rebellious to sell my soul. Not so much because I am a good person, but because I sensed that there were some ugly things hiding in the shadows around me. They had to do with me, but also with the system I was part of. The landlord, the bank, the parents, they were all not going to change their positions—why should they? They were the rightful owners of our borrowed life. They did not care about my new insights and my new voice, they were laughing at my treasure chest full of tales.

I had to finally face it: either I would give in and accept those bitter pills and the stretched-out hands to take out another loan, or I would have to drastically cut expenses and immediately reduce debts. I realized that financial strings also meant emotional costs.

We found a cheaper apartment building, I got another job, and I distanced from many people, including my parents. To live up to my inner convictions, I had to grow physically, emotionally, and mentally out of debt. I had to stop buying into the concept of wanting amenities and trading them in for a piece of my integrity.

Money and support in the following years were so scarce that I look back and wonder how we did it. How were we going to change the situation if not by breaking the rules as suggested by Campbell in "Pathways to Bliss?" This is exactly what it had boiled down to. I needed to break some rules: I always strived to be nice, sweet, and easy, but it was time for change.

Learning to Think for Myself

First, I became fed up with the intricate stories full of the strife of written myth. Were we mere toys of some destiny-shaping force, fooled by either a power outside of us or one on the inside, until we understood the name of the game? Contrary to the common opinion, I found the written myths to be complicated, too random, too confusing, and too violent for my taste. I had to admit, I disliked them. Deceitful gods and goddesses could be found everywhere in real life. Written myths seemed to model that the giving up of integrity was needed to maintain a good relation to the divine and survive on Earth. I could not believe that life should be so utterly unfair.

To gain usable know-how on what is needed for transformation to occur in real life, I expected that the monomyth, as a structured story, would give me that linear sequence: if you do A, then B occurs. As an astrologer, I wanted to be able to map out the path of a hero's transformation to find the planetary mechanism behind it. Therefore, I expected a simple but precise, linear sequence of A, then B, then C, and then D in a story, which would have to be evident also in planetary movements. When trying to tie the already complex stories to the complexity of cosmic cycles, then try to trace it in somebody's chart, the information became too mixed up and could be interpreted randomly. True, there were nuggets of wisdom everywhere, but they did not make a whole, structured story, as I expected they should. It boiled down to that I could not really identify with any of the figures in written myths, because mostly I did not like their attitude and could not understand their way of acting. They just were no material for role models, I found.

While learning to value my own observations and research just as much as other people's, I abandoned my research of the written myths because I could not find the match I had envisioned between the hero's journey and astrology. There were quite several books on the market aspiring the same, trying to connect the heroic journey to astrology, but their findings did not satisfy me either. There was no linear build-up, as I envisioned it should have. How could the hero's journey serve as a guideline if it just ended up in philosophical and psychological discourses? It did not give me the straight answers I was looking for. I wanted to know how the magic was working and how the mechanics behind it all functioned.

Timeless Wisdom in Fairy Tales

When it came to fairy tales, on the other hand, I could easily understand the heroines' motivations, feel their pain, rejoice in their journeys, and find wisdom in the rich imagery and symbols of the tales. Their lives, adventures, and longings were relatable to my own, and I realized that somehow, I had believed since childhood in a good spirit or a good fairy-godmother to help people along in life with her magic. I knew that admitting this might be admitting a bit of naivete, but I didn't mind. Wasn't my not questioning Campbell's take on the folk tales naïve? He dismissed them as old wives' tales, at best serving the child in his development, like so many before and after him had done. But I was looking at those same tales as stories filled with hidden knowledge and timeless wisdom.

For millennia, ever since writing was developed, humans have considered only written material as valuable, as if what can be written down automatically becomes *the truth*. There were other opinions out there and who was I going to believe?

Eugene Drewermann, a German theologian and psychoanalyst, argues for the value of fairy tales that they present a solution for whatever problem is posed. "They are the only kind of world literature which make us believe that love and love alone can make us happy."[9] Everywhere else in the great works of art and literature it is illustrated that who risks love will fail miserably. He states that we might think that this is how it is, that life really is nothing but misery, unjust and unfair,

9 Quote from a TV interview: "Eugen Drewermann: Eine Theologie der Märchen, Sternstunde" (Eugen Drewermann: A Theology of Fairy Tales, Star Hour Religion) , SRF Schweizer Radio und Fernsehen, 2015

because this is what is also confirmed by the daily news. But the fairy tales counter this misery with their own message. According to him, in psychoanalytical terms the kind of world we live in today would be called "highly neurotic," but he sees that books like the Bible or a collection of fairy tales can give people a way out of this brutal world. These stories have the ability to provide us, he claims, with a vision of how the violence of real life can be overcome.

I wholeheartedly agreed with him, and promised myself to now just trust my own perceptions and experiences.

The Rebellious Power of "But"

The wide range of folk tales held something in store for all kind of audiences, and I had to build a repertoire since I was on the road quite a lot now as a professional storyteller. I found the folk tales to be generally easy to learn by heart, even the long ones, because they followed a special build-up. To take the key images of the action and draw or write them in the form of a circle helped me to memorize it. It was not necessary to learn a tale like an actor would memorize his lines. Since the folk tales were from an oral heritage, they already used a natural order, which was easy to follow, if one reproduced the images along the storyline. *(Please see an example of a Fairy Tale Circle Page 44)*

However, I quickly realized that if I was trying to be more creative and change the action and images around, my audience became confused and they lost track of the story. I risked losing my listeners' attention, therefore it was best to move with the given structure. The more tales I worked with, the more the structure of the tales began to feel like a rhythm to me.

Johannes Merkel of the University of Bremen, Germany, wrote that in oral storytelling traditions what mattered all around the world was not necessarily the exact wording, nor the use of the exact same images, for that was the storytellers' freedom. What was absolutely important was the exact *order* in which the tale was told, or in other words that it kept up with the ever-recurring build-up.[10]

10 " Hören, Sehen, Staunen—Kulturgeschichte des Mündlichen Erzählens "(Listening, Seeing, Marveling—Cultural History of Oral Storytelling) by Johannes Merkel, Georg Olms Verlag, 2015

Example of a Fairy Tale Circle (used to learn a tale by heart)

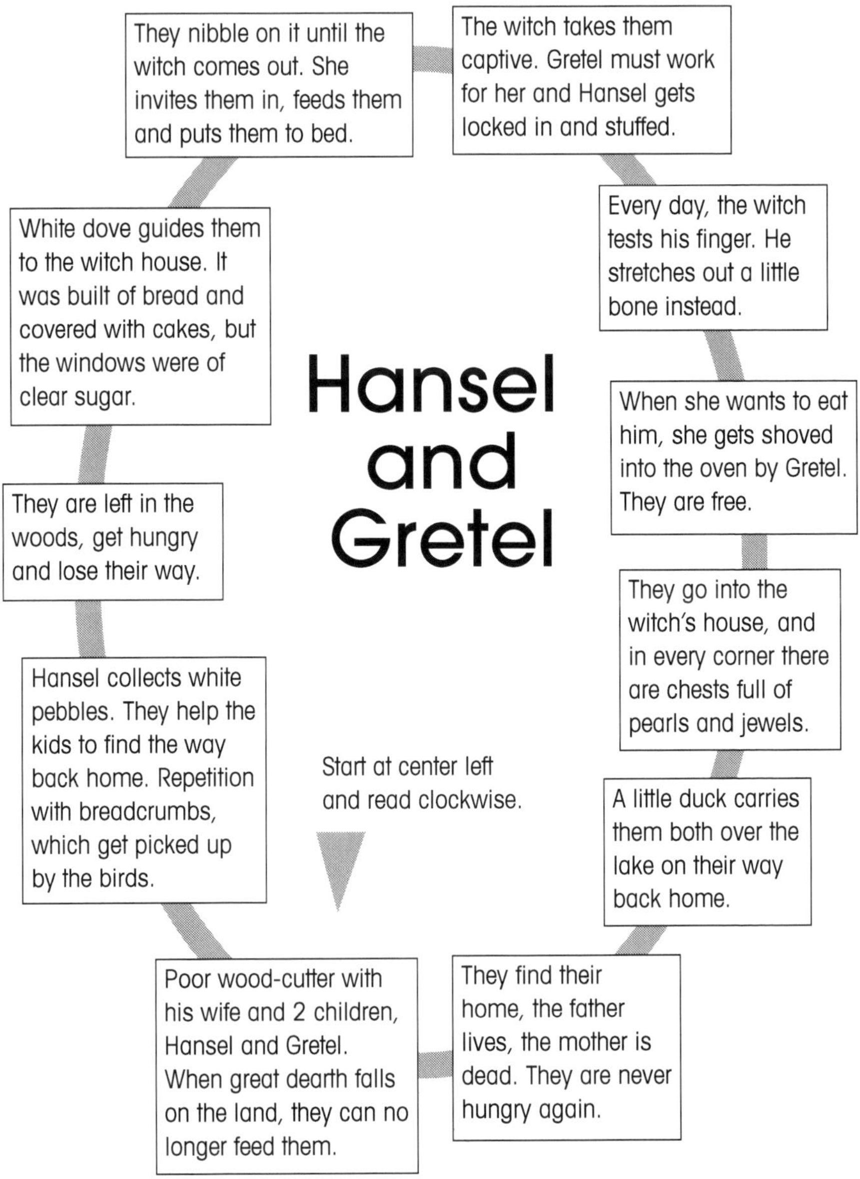

There was another thing I noticed. Often in tales, a disruptive moment was accompanied by a little word that marked a turn in destiny—the word "but." Whenever the story was going down a path where the audience almost certainly knew the outcome, it would suddenly take a turn indicated by a *but.* In "Hansel and Gretel" alone, there are twenty-five uses of the word *but* in the original English translation. This little word seemed to break up the regular linear flow of the fairy tale reality.

In the Norwegian tale "The Twelve Wild Ducks," there are thirty instances of the word *but* and the story starts out with a very impactful situation where the word *but* is used. "If I only had a daughter as white as snow and as red as blood, I shouldn't care what became of all my sons," says the queen to herself. That's quite a disruptive thought, a mother of twelve sons ready trade them in for a single daughter. It continues: "*But* the words were scarcely out of her mouth before an old troll witch came up to her. 'A daughter you shall have'… " Every time, when the story was preparing for a turn, the word *but* entered the narrative. That interjection presents the queen with the option to leave the trail of a linear, predestined life.

To our ears, the word *but* means resistance. Normally, something nice is being said, only to be ruined with a dreadful *but.* "I love your new hair, *but…*" However, after some research of this curious fact, I found that originally the word *but* stems from the West-Germanic "be-utan" and "utana" meaning *out, outside, from without*[11], thus implying that something from the outside is coming in. Now, in a fairy tale, this word

11 etymonline.com/index.php?term=but

and its attitude, seem to imply something invisible working its way into the linear destiny of the protagonists.

The word *but* obviously functions like a hinge in the story introducing something new which alters the regular course of the protagonist's path. It also often calls an otherworldly helper onto the plan, just like the old troll witch in the above-mentioned tale. Could it be that this little word can summon up an ally who had been waiting behind the red line to jump in as soon as a fairy tale figure needs help?

Many times, *but* also stands at the very beginning of a tale, implying that linear life gets interrupted and things are up for change. Destiny now takes its course and things bear an equally great potential for tragedy as for grandiosity. "*But* the queen died, and the king married a new woman. She also had a daughter the same age and one would think that the two young princesses would happily play together. *But* this was not so..." Life throws in many a *but* for young princesses in tales. However, thanks to them, the princesses have a chance to detect their inner strengths, overcome evil in cooperation with the help of spirit. There always seems to be an invisible force, which feeds and guides the heroines from behind the veil, leading them to detecting their own creativity and divinity. All of this will transform a shy and modest girl into a fair, independent, and glorious queen.

So, as I built my circular memorizing help for each new tale I learned, it became evident that especially one kind of tale, the *wonder tale*, continues throwing in all these *buts* to drive and cause the necessary changes in a story from initial trouble to happy ending. It was this little word that prevented the protagonists' destiny from going down the linear path from misery to more misery. It was all thanks to this little word, a word full of resistance, rebellion, and stubbornness that a new destiny began to weave itself for them. And as the protagonists were always deeply connected to their surroundings, their environment would get transformed right along with them.

I noticed that hidden in the fairy tales, there was always talk of an invisible realm so closely connected to our tangible plane that it kept supplying the protagonist on her path with the rebellious power of "but" and the intuitive insights she needed to change her linear path. So, the fairy tales not only spoke of encounters with invisible beings, but also of a strong invisible influence that helped shape the heroine's path and world around her.

Featuring the Invisible

People interested in stories are fascinated by the moments of transformation. They had always been fascinating to me, as well, and connected my interest in folk tales to my counseling work. Even though many of the wonder tales had similar motifs, the moment of change was still very special and feverishly awaited by the listeners.

As the land of fairy tales became even more appealing to me the more time I spent entrenched in their world, I also used fairy tale images to illustrate astrological principles in counseling sessions. Clients were hoping for transformational moments when they came to me and therefore, we would be searching their chart for indications of change. Then, we wanted to find the right attitude and plan of action that might provoke the hoped-for magic to happen. But what was it we actually were trying to get hold of? I noticed that it was something elusive, which normally was hidden from regular thinking patterns.

In fairy tales, life seems to follow a certain logic, even if it is a different logic from common everyday understanding. The invisible is featured just as much as the visible. In all the folk tales, there is an interplay of the tangible and the intangible. All is considered to have a soul, and everything is considered worth talking to.

As a child, I sat by little creeks and on mossy wood clearings, waiting to catch a glimpse of a fairy, dwarf or nymph, though it never happened. Instead I found myself talking to sparrows and ducks while I waited. Of course, any time I saw a blade of grass move for no apparent reason, or a twig trembled, I assumed there were elves or dwarfs there, I could just not see them. The folk tales delivered a worldview in which all of this was plain normal. I figured if they were as old as the Grimm Brothers assumed, thinking them to be scattered pieces of a long- lost ancient myth,[12] and they had been told and retold by every generation anew, even though they had been called lie stories, well then maybe this invisible world really did exist and was not just somebody's fantasy.

I learned that the originator of quantum theory, Max Planck, argued in one of his famous lectures that our world must be populated by what he called "spirit beings." He reasoned that behind every energy there would have to be assumed an *intelligent spirit* as a primordial source and without *spirit*, there would be no material matter. But since *spirit* as such cannot exist per se either, but rather must belong to

12 "Wie alt sind unsere Märchen?"(How Old are Fairy Tales?), Herausgeberin: Europäische Märchengesellschaft e.V., Rheine, 1990

a being, we are compelled to accept "spirit beings." [13] So here I had an explanation of what I felt was true and what was reflected in the folk tales. More so, quantum mechanics says that our material universe is part of an invisible energy matrix, which together forms a field in which all is at interplay with one another.[14] Isn't this exactly what the folk tales talk about all the time? The heroines distinguish themselves from normal figures by displaying their connectedness to the field; for them it is a matter of fact. On their journeys, they are always in exchange with their surroundings, paying close attention to what and who is there and what is being conveyed to them. By watching and reacting they are at interplay with the *intelligent spirit* and thus actively contributing to more options on their path.

So, the fairy tale protagonists need to be able to discern well. The folk tales model the interaction between the protagonist and its surroundings. Often it is the fairy tale heroine, who is the one stepping into a dialogue, while in contrast her two stepsisters or his two older brothers disregard the encounters as worthless.

The originators of the tales lived long before modern quantum physics could explain this, still they spoke of a kind of *motherly* support through nature's spirit helpers, which is activated as soon as the protagonist takes on the attitude that there is a *creative force* behind everything. They saw *the divine* shine through everything, which they believed to be a *she*, because bringing forth new life was a feminine capacity.

---

13 "Archiv zur Geschichte der Max-Planck-Gesellschaft"(Archive on the History of the Max Planck Society) , Abt. Va, Rep. 11 Planck, Nr. 1797

14 "Spontaneous Evolution: Our Positive Future and a Way to Get There From Here, " Bruce H. Lipton, Ph.D. and Steve Bhaerman, Hay House, 2009

In folk tales, the helpers of this creative force are *nature spirits*. Their task is to tend to the growth and well-being of all life on the planet: humans, animals, plants, rocks, minerals—every material thing on the face of the Earth as vast or tiny as it might be. Everything on the material plane is subject to birth and decay, comings and goings. As a logical conclusion, nothing stands in value above the other and everything is sacred, everything is ensouled and moved by a *spirit being*, just like Max Planck stated. Everything is in a give-and-take-relationship with one another and the effects of this become visible on our material plane and in our human destiny.

The Otherworld, Home of Spirit and the Divine

Adam, the Celtic healer in Ross Heaven's books[15], calls the material realm we live in "God's visible face." He reminds his disciple that the divine can only be detected by its effects on the material world. Living life from such a viewpoint is the language of the folk tales.

So, according to them, the invisible world is the dwelling place of the *intelligent spirit*. It often gets called "the otherworld." All tangible things in our realm stem from that *other* world, which is rather hidden behind a veil. Fairy tales report of gates opening at certain times, like for example at midnight during what we recognize as the Christmas season (which must have been the winter solstice in pre-Christian times) when

15 "The Sin Eater's Last Confessions, Lost Traditions of Celtic Shamanism " and "Walking with the Sin Eater, A Celtic Pilgrimage on the Dragon Path," Ross Heaven, Llewellyn Worldwide, Ltd, 2008/2010

suddenly the human is allowed into the mountain to take a peak of the treasures normally concealed from the human eye.

The tales always model this relationship between the invisible and the visible, the human and the otherworld. Without this exchange, there would be no life on the planet.

A German tale also speaks of the time around Christmas, when a young farmer carried out a little ritual, which he had learned from his forefathers, to call back the creative forces in nature, the light at the winter solstice. He calls *Mother Hulda*, or *Mother Holle*, who was the goddess of our ancestors, to awaken the Earth.[16]

Mother Hulda blesses the Earth

Again, it was Christmas time. A young farmer put on his warm coat and boots and pulled his cap deep down over his ears and stepped down into his orchard. He did what he had seen his father and his grandfather do for many years, when they were still alive. First, he shook an apple tree so that the snow fell on his shoulders in a fine dust, then he went over to a pear tree muttering, "Little tree, little tree, wake up, Mother Hulda is coming!" Suddenly, he heard a subtle rustling, felt a sudden stir in the air and snow was whirling around his face. In a white cloud he saw Mother Hulda standing in front of him, changing into a white dove before his eyes. She flew up, once around the pear tree, then she flew over to the apple tree, encircling it and then she flew over all closed buds and around every single tree in the orchard. Then she flew without a sound over the whole garden,

16 This ancient goddess was called by many different names. In Germany, for example, she was *Frau Holle*, in Sweden, she was called *Huldra*.

and further on to the farmer's fields. A bright glow seemed to accompany her flight over the bushes and the trees, the fields and the acres. With her wings she was awakening the bulbs and roots slumbering deep down underneath their snowy blanket. The farmer knew that now they could sprout again, that they would grow in springtime, as soon as the sun would warm the earth and melt the snow. He also knew that where the dove had landed and rested, the most gorgeous flowers would unfold their blossoms to cheer everybody's heart.

Here, the intangible gets named and depicted. The divine appears as the man's goddess in a white cloud and then changes into a white dove, awakening nature's slumbering creative force. You might argue that nature awakens every year without humans performing any rites. But still, a vast love for all things shines through in this tale. The young farmer loves his garden, the trees, and the fields, and by doing this ritual, he gets to witness the workings of the divine.

To witness the workings of the divine can touch us at our very core. I noticed that if I walked through my life in this state of awe, marveling at "God's visible face, life became so much richer. When considering the trees, the dirt, the small and large critters, all of nature around me, bliss could be made to return to my life. This is where in my eyes the concept of God became tangible, but it was not tied to a gender or a religion. I was convinced the fact that folk tales portray this otherwise invisible activity of the divine contributed to their positive impact.

When the protagonist of a fairy tale interacts with nature, nature responds. Such is an animistic way of perceiving the world, as it can be found in indigenous cultures from all over the planet. It seems to be a natural consequence of living close to nature and her cycles. Since we all were indigenous at one time or another in history, the animistic way of looking at life seems to be deeply rooted as an innate knowing in our human experience.

Imogen Seger, a German-American sociologist poses an interesting question: *"How, if not in human words, should humans speak of something, which is not comprehensible to them? And how should they not experience only a little bit of what is incomprehensible to them, if they do not speak about it?"*[17]

17 "Wenn die Geister Wiederkehren, Weltdeutung und Religiöses Bewusstsein in Primitiven Kulturen" (When the Spirits Recur, World Interpretation and Religious Consciousness in Primitive Cultures), Imogen Seger, Piper 1982

Chapter 4

Web of Lies or Web of Dreams?

"Nature is the visible face of spirit and will always reveal the truth to us."
Ross Heaven

As I was exploring the worldview of folk tales, I also tried to understand their magic. It seemed that viewing one's surrounding as ensouled would allow for a certain collaboration with the creative forces. After all, couldn't we all need a good dose of transformational magic?

While getting out of unhealthy dependencies, I started to question many things in life. There seemed to be some wrong mechanism in our modern society. I was disagreeing with people left and right, especially with my parents, and my support system dwindled at a fast rate. I was clearly taking a stand for personal freedom and equal relationships, but my surroundings seemed to want to prove me wrong.

What struck me was that on a closer look friends and friends of friends were all enslaved by debts far worse than we were, working day and night to pay off their houses and cars, while their families broke under the pressure. But since the economy was in crisis in those years, economists repeatedly advised people to *increase* their consumption, because the more the consumers bought, the sooner the economy would regenerate. This meant that a *good* citizen was a *consuming* citizen. No wonder the environment got competitive and everybody only looked after himself. What had we gotten ourselves into? What rules was our society playing by instead of being supportive of each other?

I observed that in their misery, friends and clients were desperately asking themselves: "Why is this happening to me?" While I think it's good to be self-reflective, I also thought that there was something bigger going on in our society. We were all collectively caught in a trap. We were sacrificing our own happiness to contribute to the wealth of a few ruthless people, who were growing richer at the cost of our personal integrity. It seemed like a modern form of slavery. We spent money we didn't own, but at the same time, we were enticed and encouraged to do so. Slowly but surely, we became indebted to the lenders as we amassed things, we couldn't afford, and in consequence we lost our independence and personal power. And we were even asked to further increase this unhealthy behavior. We were contributing to a *web of lies* here! It was time that we finally stopped doing what we were told. The idea of ownership in nature started to preoccupy me.

Adam, the Celtic healer in Ross Heaven's book, tells his disciple that, *"People make their own blockages—which usually amount to a fear of owning their power. Then, before they know it, their lives have slipped away, and it is too late for them to act because they are caught in the web of lies."*[18] If we all would start to own our power and not let our lives slip

18 "The Sin Eater's Last Confessions, Lost Traditions of Celtic Shamanism," Ross Heaven, Llewellyn Worldwide, 2008, p. 106

away, we might get out of such a web of lies and gain back our integrity and freedom. I know they are big words, and this is said easily, but it got me thinking, especially as I was just working on an article using a local folk tale called "The Greedy Farmer".

The Greedy Farmer

Once upon a time, there was a large famine in the land. The winter was long and hard, and people's pantries were empty. A wealthy farmer, however, still had a large stock of potatoes in his cellar, but since he was the only one in the entire area who still had potatoes, he wanted to keep them and sell them as seed-potatoes in springtime. He knew he would then be able to ask for the highest price ever. Every day, people came knocking on his door, asking for some of his potatoes to feed their starving children, but neighbor or not, he did not give in to their pleas. He also did not give to those who wanted to buy from him.

When springtime came, the farmer contently descended into his basement to fetch his potatoes, but there was a giant, ugly toad sitting on the heap. Each and every potato had turned as green as grass, the entire heap was spoiled and couldn't even be given to the pigs. The farmer had to toss them all out.

The wisdom of this short tale is clear. It is Mother Nature's law and will that her abundance not be greedily hoarded by one person but shared to sustain all her children. He was contributing to the *web of lies*, propped up by the idea that nature's gifts can be owned, that some people are more deserving than others and that there is not enough for everybody. This stands in stark contrast to how benevolent nature would be if all had access to its abundance. The farmer seems to have forgotten that it is essential for all beings to be in exchange with their environment.

No one is isolated on this planet. No single being can survive without the exchange with the outside. Even the most basic body functions like breathing and eating require an exchange between us and the world we live in. Being isolated is as if we were holding our breaths and forgetting to exhale. Life *renews* itself through the constant exchange between inside and outside, between the single person and the collective. By exhaling, what was inside is sent back out again to contribute to the atmosphere of the outside world. This is how it would be natural. After inhaling and keeping the breath in for a little while, it is a natural reflex to let it out again. Life is a give and take in all matters.

So, if this "breathing rhythm" is to the depletion of some, while others keep it all in, there is a mess up in the balance, isn't there? I noticed that many a tale spoke of exactly this imbalance, but also gave instructions on how the balance could be regained.

Let's take "Hansel and Gretel" as an example. Hansel could first ask himself, "Why is this happening to me?" and might conclude having not been a good enough boy. He could try to be a better one. Then he could start to blame his mother for his hunger and misery. But tales never state such things, because if Hansel had dwelled in a blame and resignation mode, he and his sister would have long ago perished from hunger, as victims of an unjust society. That would have truly been a pity, since the children would have missed the chance to grow back into alignment with the natural laws.

Hansel was smart. First, he started to look around to find solutions. By leaving the bread crumbs, he got into contact with the birds in the woods, even though unwillingly at first, but this seemed to open the interaction between him and the creative forces. We know that *Mother Holle* can appear as a bird, and indeed, in the middle of their misery, a snow-white bird appears and guides the children deep into Mother Nature's unspoiled natural realm, the dark deep woods.

They began to walk again, but they always came deeper into the forest, and if help did not come soon, they must die of hunger and weariness. When it was mid-day, they saw a beautiful snow-white bird sitting on a bough, which sang so delightfully that they stood still and listened to it. And when its song was over, it spread its wings and flew away before them, and they followed it until they reached a little house, on the roof of which it alighted.

The forester and author Peter Wohlleben writes about the harmonizing effect on being in the woods from a scientific stand point. In the woods, people get exposed to substances which are produced by the trees that contribute to their general well-being, strengthening the immune system, and lowering their blood pressure.[19]

So, in the deep woods, the creative force is relentlessly bringing forth sustenance and abundance, good and healthy things for people. So, Hansel and Gretel start to heal in Mother Nature's wooden realm. This mother of all would not let her children starve, but first, they needed to regain their strength to survive, as we will see in Chapter 7. Had Hansel chosen to view himself as isolated and alone and not gotten

19 See the English edition: "The Hidden Life of Trees: What They Feel, How They Communicate—Discoveries from a Secret World," Peter Wohlleben, Greystone books, 2016

into contact with his surroundings, these two children would have not made it. In the end they even found the witch's treasure chest, now they would never go hungry again.

Figuratively, Hansel and Gretel have found the key to nature's horn of plenty. It is the key to what the Celtic healer Adam calls the *web of dreams*. However, in a web of lies they got cut off from the divine creative forces, the laws of Mother Nature, and in the end of the tale they found their way back into the web of dreams, which is *the way home*. Or as Adam explains to his disciple: *"There is a web of dreams and a web of lies that we can give our energy to. One will take us home and one will leave us hanging."*[20]

This all got me to thinking. Was this question merely to be answered on an individual level or were there rules which stood above human-made laws and regulations? The folk tales offered me a window into a world where injustices were pointed out and then remedied. Unfair became fair and power situations got balanced out until all was well again.

A Window into Another Worldview

Soon I received the opportunity to immerse myself even deeper in the fairy tale world. I was supposed to write a series of articles about Swiss folk tales for a folklore magazine, which at the same time was going to be printed in a hip Swiss travel magazine. I was asked to approach the folk tales from a completely different angle, because the articles did *not* ask for a metaphorical or psychological explanation, something which I

20 "The Sin Eater's Last Confessions, Lost Traditions of Celtic Shamanism," Ross Heaven, Llewellyn Worldwide, 2008, p. 51

was used to, *but* rather for local tales brought into context with a place to visit or a hiking route. It was one of these "buts" which turned out to be a hinge in my life, for had this article series not pushed me to examine the folk tales from a new perspective, this book would have never been written. I was asked to think very much outside of my regular frame of mind.

Folk tales are considered outside of time and space, somewhat elusive and universal, and are not to be tied down to a single place and a time in the real world. Still, they often do name a place in their narration. Though considering that in every region anywhere in Europe the same kind of story motifs occur, a specific location name might not be of so much value after all. Folk tales always come with the air of, "*It could have happened or not, here or any place else.*" For example, the above tale of the greedy farmer originally begins with, "*In Uri, a wealthy farmer still had a large stock of potatoes in the year of the great hunger of 1817*", as if it were a report of actual events, which it is. In Central Europe, there was a famine of tremendous proportions during that exact year. Weather conditions two years before, cold winters, very late springs, and cool summers, led to bad harvests. The following winter, the grain prices quadrupled in Switzerland and there was scarcity everywhere. Forty to fifty percent of the population died.[21]

Did tales now speak of facts, or of metaphorical things, or both? So, there was an actual event, but wasn't its message also timeless? While a tale could very well be talking of actual events, at a specific place and time in history, it most definitely also contained a mysterious element

21 "Hearth & Home, a History of Material Culture," Norman J.G. Pounds, Indiana University Press, 1989, p. 234

that was timeless. This aspect of the story gave evidence of another worldview, a belief where *a toad* interfered in the wrongdoings of a greedy man. This also must then be the reason why such a story landed in a collection of tales and not in a history book. In people's minds, the toad seemed to have something to do with the potatoes going bad. It seemed to represent Mother Nature, who acts as a guardian of her gifts which were not to be misused for selfish reasons. Was here the key to understanding the concept of *a web of dreams* versus *a web of lies*? Humans who owned the power they were naturally given and used it wisely were acting in alignment with Mother Nature and therefore contributed to creating a web of dreams, a life of harmony and freedom for all. Whereas those who hoarded and were greedy contributed to a web of lies, they lived off the misery of others.

I needed to further explore the folk tale's way of looking at life and I soon got a chance to do so.

Chapter 5

The Pumpkin Birth

"Faeries come take me out of this dull world,
For I would ride with you upon the wind,
Run on the top of the disheveled tide,
And dance upon the mountains like a flame."
William Butler Yeats

Both of our children were in a camp one weekend, so my husband and I made reservations in a hotel up in the mountains. Since I needed to hand in suggestions for the article series, I had brought a stack of Swiss folk tales of the region we were going to visit. Maybe I could combine our mini-vacation with some research *sur place*. Our hotel was in beautiful Leysin, which is located at the foot of a massive rock, the Tour d'Aï. The hotel room was spacious, and the view was stunning. The leaves had already started to turn yellow and washed the scenery with a golden glow. The air was crisp and made the tip of the Dent du Midi on the opposite side of the Rhone Valley look crystal clear and seem very close. Soon, the entire mountain range was going to be covered by the first snow.

I made myself comfortable on a sofa by the window and started to read the tales I had brought with me. The first was a Swiss tale exactly from this area by the name of "The Three Languages", a tale which the Grimm Brothers had included in their collection. It is about a young man, Hans, who had learned to speak the language of animals, much to his father's disapproval. It turned out, though, that Hans's capacity to understand the barking of dogs, the croaking of frogs, and the birds' chirping led him to become the pope in the end. On our way up to Leysin, we passed the area where this tale originated. Now the river Rhone flowed in a neat and straight riverbed, but not too long ago the area was a huge marshland. There were so many frogs in it that the locals up until recently gave each other nicknames containing the word "frog" or "toad." Nobody could say how long this already had been going on, but it remained a nice little anecdote. People from *Ollons* called their neighbors in *Aigle* "les renoillards(the frogs)" while those did not hesitate to call people from *Ollons* "les boïards(the toads)". My husband and I chuckled at the idea that for people living here, understanding the language of frogs must have been not so farfetched. Again, there was also a more serious and timeless message transmitted by the tale: Whoever can understand what animals and nature have to say is going to be a leader, and for the Catholic population of that area, the highest leader is the pope. As opposed to the greedy farmer, Hans listened and understood.

This tale, too, seemed to be a combination of historical names and places while at the same time also containing a somewhat otherworldly message. Not only was it beyond regular human capacity to understand animals, but it also was a twist in fate that Hans got elected pope. I was fascinated by this mixing of the supernatural with the regular world. It was his understanding the animals and reacting to what they said in the physical world that made his destiny change. His predetermined fate would have actually been to be a shepherd. But by actively interacting with his environment and not just passively dreaming of a better life, his fate changed "magically."

I got up from the sofa and stretched myself in front of the window. The view was gorgeous, clear blue sky behind snow-white mountain peaks. A bright orange coach with Asian tourists had just arrived and they now were pouring into the lobby. I still had a half an hour before dinner, so I chose to read another tale, one from *Lötschental* about pumpkins. It probably also caught my eye because the bright orange hue of pumpkins was shining right next to the entrance of the hotel as they were stacked up there for decoration. The pumpkins came from *Valais*, just like the tale, which again was right around the corner from the Rhone Delta.

The Pumpkin Birth

The people from Lötschental wanted to have a scribe, just like the other villages had. They held a council and decided to send delegates down to the Rhone Valley with the order to find a scribe. They assumed that a scribe would be born into this world like a chicken out of an egg, and so they went to the market. Upon seeing a large, round pumpkin, they figured it must be exactly such an egg. They asked the vendor, "Are these the eggs out of which scribes are hatched?" The vendor nodded, and the delegates bought the pumpkin. It was a heavy pumpkin and it took them quite a long time to carry it back to their village in the Lötschental, high up in the mountains. There they positioned it on the market place and three were called on to hatch it. Two of them sat on either side of the pumpkin and the third one on top. But it so happened that suddenly, when they rotated their position, the pumpkin started to roll. It rolled and rolled down the hill until it finally came to a halt in the bushes, where it startled a hare. The hare took flight and the astonished men called out: "Our scribe has hatched! Our scribe has hatched!" And when they saw the hare's long ears, they nodded in a satisfied manner: "Just see, the quill is already behind his ear."

Lötschental is a remote mountain valley known for its strong traditions and rustic folklore. Especially during Carnival, the hidden valley attracts many tourists, because people there put on large, scary, wooden masks and dress all in fur, skin, and rags. By doing that, they seem to be shapeshifting into another time and age when paganism was stronger than Christianity. Even the tourists get drawn into this other world. It could well have been a world where people believed things were born out of pumpkins. Was this tale conveying such an old worldview?

That evening over a candle-light dinner in Leysin, there was much for us to talk about. The restaurant was cozy and somewhat old-fashioned, in a rustic chalet style. Fondue and raclette were served, typical local dishes. It was the perfect setting to dive into a discussion about the beliefs of our forefathers. Did people really think one could learn the language of animals and that things were born out of pumpkins? What an interesting concept this was. We tried very hard to see the world through mountain-valley people's eyes, people who believed humans were born from eggs the size of golden pumpkins. But how far back into the past did we have to go? One hundred years or a thousand? If we were touching on paganism, it would have had to be prior to the introduction of Christianity. In remote areas, however, where people lived a simple life close to nature, we knew that the belief in nature's magic existed up until very recently side-by-side with the Christian church. In fact, the pastor had to accept that his flock put bowls of cream for the little people out on the windowsill and that they expected to meet Mother Hulda in the woods on their way to church. Also, he had to consider that they were afraid to be drawn into the lake by water spirits or enchanted by fairies. Only industrialization, radio, electricity, and TV started to put an end to this and brought the modern age to their world. This was as recent as the 1940s.[22]

We compared it to our road trip in the United States where we were without TV for six months, when we quickly came into close contact with our natural surroundings. We, too, had the desire to talk to the animals we encountered—or at least to understand them. Somehow, everything held magic and we wanted to become part of it. However, once the trip was over and we told friends in the modern world about it, they could not quite understand what we were talking about. We also were not able to keep up this somewhat enchanted outlook on life once we were back in the buzz of daily life. Maybe it was the same with the remote Lötschberg people versus those down in the Rhone Valley, where travelers had always been passing through for centuries, if not millennia, moving goods, ideas, and news from France to Italy. The modern age certainly came sooner to the valley people, and the pumpkin tale became a mocking story about the backward living mountain people.

22 See Dr. Gerald Thomas's anthropological studies "The Two Traditions: The Art of Storytelling Amongst French Newfoundlanders," Breakwater Books Ltd., 1993

We could have left it at this, but my husband threw in, "Isn't it funny that pumpkins do somehow resemble eggs?" Yes, he was right, many fairy tales spoke about wondrous golden eggs. They were more valuable than anything and it was *the* thing to have. Oh, and what about Cinderella's pumpkin carriage? You could say that Cinderella was hatched into a princess, while riding it. The pumpkin definitely had something to do with her change back and forth between her old self, the abused stepdaughter, and her new self, a princess.

Early the next morning, we went up to the *Tour d'Aï*, the large rock towering above Leysin, to get a feel for another tale from this area. However, upon arriving there, we were utterly disappointed. No fairy tale romance was to be found there. Large slopes with scree between huge power pylons had taken over where there once must have been lush meadows. Nature was being tamed here for people to ski, just as the Rhone River had been canalized where there once had been marshland. The wilderness of the mountain was forced to make room for modern life. Still, we detected the little lake mentioned in the tale and spotted some cows and shelters for people and cattle. The shelters indicated that even though nature could be tamed by humans to a certain degree, the weather still was not to be subdued. We sat down on one of the wooden benches and leaned our backs against the shelter. The sun was mild on this gorgeous fall day and I took out my book of tales and began reading aloud how in this exact place a mortal once met a fairy.

Michel and Nérine

Once upon a time there were good fairies living in the Tour d'Aï, a gigantic rock towering behind the little Lac d'Aï. They helped the shepherds and saved many an animal from falling from the steep rocks. The herdsmen were grateful and thanked them by putting out a dish with fresh golden cream every night in front of their huts. It so happened that Nérine, the youngest of the fairies, fell in love with a handsome blond shepherd. Michel was not only very handsome and diligent, he also had a very good heart and sang on every occasion.

One day, when he was out hunting alone, suddenly, in a lonely valley, the fairy stood in front of him. Michel came to a stop and immediately was enraptured by her beauty. Her hair was long and black and was rustled by the wind. It didn't take long and the two of them were talking and joking. At one point Nérine wanted to know, "What is happiness for you?" and he answered, "Beautiful meadows and a nice herd. And the favor of you fairies. And good health." "Nothing more?" the fairy wanted to know. "Well, of course," he said, and blushed, "Also good friends and a loving wife." Nérine raised her wand, touched a nearby rose and said, "All of this you can have, Michel." And in front of his eyes, the rose changed into a winged chariot. Hundreds of swallows came flying and let themselves be bridled with golden strings. Nérine invited Michel into the chariot and up in the air they flew. In the meantime, night had fallen, and beneath them the mountain, the rocks, the woods and the meadows and valleys lay in darkness, while the creeks and lakes were shimmering in the moonlight. Michel was so enchanted by this flight with the lovely fairy that soon his heart and his voice began to sing. After what felt like an eternity (or just a short moment, he couldn't tell), the fairy steered the winged chariot to the Tour d'Aï and had it land softly on a meadow. From then on, they regularly met for nightly flights across the mountains and valleys. Nérine even showed her lover the glittering crystal cave in which she lived with the other fairies, and its treasures of gold and silver. However, Michel's heart grew heavy upon the thought that he would have to decide between living with the fairies in this cave and flying by night, and his life in daylight on the fragrant meadows with his cows and among his fellow humans.

By this time, Michel's friends were growing weary of his nocturnal excursions and there were rumors. Judith, a farmer's daughter from down in the village, heard of it, and since she was in love with Michel, too, she decided to put an end to this thing. Full of bitter love, she convinced one of the shepherds to rub the bowl for the fairies with the poisonous gentian flower, before putting cream in it. It was known that the fairies hated the smell of this plant. The shepherd did as he was told and in the very same night, a piercing scream resounded through the valley. The next morning, the shepherds found the bowl shattered and the cream spilled on the floor. From that day on, neither Nérine nor any other of the fairies were ever seen again. Life for the herdsmen became hard and difficult. Cows lost their way and fell from the steep rocks, and hail and thunderstorms swept across the mountains. Some said that the disappointed fairies had moved to a wood near Les Diablerets. Many a times Michel and his friends looked up to the Tour d'Aï, which now was empty, and wondered, "Will the fairies ever return?"

We turned around on our bench and looked up at the *Tour d'Aï*. So, this was an abandoned fairy castle? It didn't take much imagination to see how this could be. "If I were a fairy, I would want to live here," I told my husband, and he nodded. How majestic was the rock which towered over us and how lush the meadows were up there, where it was too steep for humans to go. At the tower's foot, the little blue lake was shimmering like a sapphire in the fall sun. For a little while, we felt very close to those olden times, when the fairies still lived here, helping out the shepherds. I remembered that I had read some other Swiss tales where dwarfs or fairies worked hand-in-hand tending the animals in this dangerous terrain. And many a tale ended on such a bitter note as the one of Michel and Nérine. Had only jealousy not ruined the caring relationship between fairies and humans.

As our short trip was coming to an end, I slowly started to get a feeling for the folk tales' way of looking at life. Besides I could see some interesting articles emerge from this material.

Chapter 6

A Fairy in the Wood of my Childhood

"There are, however, some questions that one who is to speak about fairy-stories must expect to answer, or attempt to answer, whatever the folk of Faërie may think of his impertinence."

J.R.R. Tolkien

My articles series started to take on shape and the deeper I got into the world of folk tales, the more I felt that it was taking me into a different way of looking at life. It was a magical outlook, where indeed all beings were ensouled and toads were not merely toads, but incarnated guardians of Mother Nature. They were not toads or frogs because of some evil witch, rather they represented the goddess and could even take on human shape. I found a Swiss tale where a frog transformed herself into a pretty girl after having become friends with a nice young man. Upon her wondrous transformation she said: "I was the queen of frogs and I noticed how good you were, especially to your mother. For this reason, I came to ask you whether you wanted to marry me." I was delighted with the folk tale treasure I found in all parts and languages of Switzerland. Yet, in remote places or border areas, there seemed to be an extraordinary number.

The place I lived in was the last German-speaking community before the gates of the mostly French-speaking town of Fribourg. Beyond the town of Fribourg lies the Swiss French side of the country. At this language border, people suffered for centuries under the two opposing powers of Berne and Lausanne. The poor farmers were regularly oppressed by either the Swiss Germans or the Swiss French. A wealth of fairy tales was conserved here and collected as recent as in the 1960s. Up to that point in time, the tales were all still only in people's memories and only passed on orally. To them, the invisible belonged to their reality just as much as the visible. In our local newspaper I found an article which reported that not long ago, the sales contract for a mountain cabin near Gruyère still included this sentence: "This cabin is acquired with all seen and unseen things."

It meant that this worldview indeed had not been gone too long. So maybe not all is lost yet, I was thinking to myself, and dedicated myself fully to the recovery of this old world. I did not know that my enthusiasm was calling adversaries to the scene. But were they coming from the fairy folk trying to protect their realm or from human beings who protected their beliefs?

A Stone Fountain Called Glass Fountain

There was a mysterious fountain in the nearby woods, the *Bremgarten Wood,* where I used to play with my Scout buddies in the 1970s. It was called "The Glass Fountain." Many spooky legends of treasures and ghosts were circulating about it, but as a kid, what I found most puzzling about that fountain was that it was by no means made of *glass*, rather it was just a regular, dull, old stone fountain.

Now, for my article series I came across a tale by the name "The Glass Fountain" and it talked exactly about this fountain in the woods of my childhood. People use the wood as a recreational area, since it is right outside of Berne, despite a major highway cutting right through it. They walk their dogs, bike, or jog. It is even a place of archeological interest, and somewhere amid a labyrinth of little trails, in the heart of it, there lies this mysterious fountain. Nobody can explain its fancy name. Some claim that it is because the water is crystal clear and has healing powers.

I wanted to find out more about this stone fountain and its legends. At the same time, I wanted to shed some light on this childhood mystery of mine. It was going to be a milestone in my understanding age and worldview of folk tales.

The Glass Fountain

Once upon a time, there was a beautiful maid living in a castle. She rejected all suitors who came to the castle to propose to her, because none of them was rich enough. However, there was this one young man, who she secretly liked a lot. He was the son of a fairy.

One day, they were sitting by a well in the woods and she told him, "I know you cannot offer me a princely throne, but if you build a fountain full of gems here at this well, I will be your bride." The mother of the young man, the fairy, followed the wish of her son and conjured up a gorgeous basin in bright blue, yellow, and crimson where the well had been.

Upon seeing this stunningly beautiful fountain, the maid was very happy. But she turned to the young man again and said, "Don't you think that the woods surrounding this fountain need to become a luxurious garden, too?" Again, the fairy conjured up true splendor around the fountain, where before there had been only wood. Ah, it was lush with flowers and bushes blooming in all colors. The maid's heart sang with joy when she saw it the next morning. In the evening, the two young lovers sat again by the fountain and enjoyed each other's company. But when the maid's gaze fell upon her castle, she said, "Don't you think that the old walls need some shimmering pearls and rubies to match the garden?"

The fairy, upon hearing this, became very angry. She instantly let all the splendor vanish. The lush garden was turned back into shrubs and woods, but the glass fountain remained. Here, the young maiden sat and waited every evening, but in vain, because her lover never came. His mother had shown him his bride's proud heart. So, there she sits by the fountain of glass and waits and waits, and if she is not dead, she is still waiting.

The tale as such gave no explanation as to why the *stone* fountain was called a *glass* fountain. A tale in any case is viewed by people as nothing more than just that—a legend. Nobody would ever take its content literally. Metaphorically, it reminded young maidens not to be vain and greedy. This would make for a boring article, though, and did not answer my question. So, I had to dig a little deeper.

What if I looked at the tale as if it were a newspaper report about what happened in the woods recently? The facts would be:

- There is a stone fountain by the puzzling name "Glass Fountain."
- There is a castle in the woods, near the fountain.
- A young girl lives in it, who wants to marry a powerful, rich man.
- A fairy and her son live in those woods, too.
- The fairy is very powerful, she creates and destroys.
- Gemstones in blue, yellow, and crimson and a garden are conjured up and then disappear.

As a kid I played in those woods almost every Saturday with my Scout buddies. I remember the highway being built, and I remember the fountain, but was there any castle or ruins of an old castle? Not to my knowledge. Had there been one, we most definitely would have included the place in our playing. So, I took out a map and indeed, not far from the Glass Fountain, a place in the middle of the woods was called "Nägelischlössli," with "Schlössli" meaning "little castle" and "Nägeli" the flower "carnation." It referred to some kind of flower castle. How exciting! Encouraged, I searched on and found an online report of an archeologist who spoke about the remnants of a Celtic settlement exactly in that area of the woods.[23] Nowadays, he pointed out, it was all covered with shrubs and woods, but the remnants of the ditch and walls could still be made out.

---

23 Now available in a book: "Die Ursprünge Berns" (The Origins of Bern) by Christoph Pfister, 2013

At the next opportunity, my family and I headed out into the Bremgarten Wood to find these remnants. On the way to the fountain, I told my family the story and what we were looking for. I cannot say who was more excited, my little daughter, my husband with compass and map in hand, me, or our happy, tail-wagging dog. But arriving at the stony Glass Fountain, my daughter, too, was disappointed. It was merely a common fountain, no shimmering fountain of glass, as she had expected. It was in a nice place in the middle of the woods; however, no signs of treasures were here. "Maybe we need to come back at night," she suggested.

The search could begin not far from the fountain. We compared the archeologist's maps with the terrain, looking for mounds and ditches in the middle of the woods. All was, of course, covered with trees, shrubs, and thorns. Who would think that a little rise in the middle of the woods could be a two-and-a-half-thousand-year-old Celtic settlement? We felt like we were looking for Sleeping Beauty's enchanted castle, as we fought our way through the thick blackberry thorns. Finally, after what seemed hours, with the help of my husband's orienteering and compass skills, we were able to make out the mounds and ditches. No castle walls here. We investigated the ground closer to the site, which on the map bore the word "castle" in its name, and found that, without bushes or trees it lay in visual range of the fountain. Our dog behaved as if she was a police dog sniffing the ground for evidence, then my daughter suddenly shouted: "Come see, here is something!" And indeed, what she had found were the small remnants of a wall, only ankle-high, but clearly belonging to a man-made wall going in a straight line. We followed it and noticed that it could be made out as a small rectangle. They really were the barely recognizable ruins of somebody's long-ago house! It must have been a small dwelling, more like a cabin than a castle. Was this the vain girl's "castle?" Well, a home is said to be somebody's castle, regardless of how small, right? Together, we tried to re-establish the scene of the tale: There once was a young Celtic girl who dreamed of a better life but missed out on all her chances by being too vain. Whoever told the story later would start to blow it up a bit, adding some color and increasing the scale from a shack to a castle, from a regular girl to a princess.

Excited as we were about having found the walls, the mounds and ditches, my little daughter brought up the point: "But mommy, we still don't know why it is called a glass fountain, if it is only out of stone." True, we had found evidence that there might be some realistic foundation to the tale, however, it still gave no explanation for the fountain's name.

Back home, I began to retrace the tale's history. Evidently, before it had been included in a Swiss fairy tale collection by Otto Sutermeister in the mid-1800s, the story was in the form of a ballad—a medieval ballad, that is. I learned that medieval troubadours often performed old Celtic story material, which they adapted to their own time. This would absolutely fit our notion that somebody had exaggerated a bit with the size and shape of a castle. The word "castle" might be the equivalent of a Celtic cabin but could certainly pass for a medieval dwelling.

Luckily, the ballad soon was to be found in an archive. It was long and very dynamic—I loved it. The rhymes reflected the growing tension between the insatiable young maiden, her lover, and the fairy. Line after line, it built up a dramatic suspense, first painting a romantic scenery of glittering gemstones and lush gardens, then it all changed with the thundering entrance of the angry fairy. It was the moment of the maiden's downfall. She had asked for too much and her punishment was going to be severe. Accompanied by a thunderstorm, it came down upon her.

And suddenly lightning flames up,
In ember the sky swims,
The storm's roaring legions
In a terrible teeming throng.
The thunder rolls and bursts
It cracks the Earth's deepest foundations.

The ballad speaks of a cloud coming down and lulling the fairy's son into a slumber, carrying him out and away. It continues:

In its stead now appears the Fairy in her dragon chariot.

Wild with anger, the fairy makes everything disappear and starts to punish the girl. The maiden is condemned to enjoy the fountain and the garden *alone* night after night at midnight, until a pure lovers' first kiss is given.

That was quite an example of dramatic storytelling, for medieval bards obviously knew their craft.[24]

---

24 Bards were the carriers of a long tradition, which went back at least to Celtic times, as we know from Roman texts. They were trained in "the magic of sound, using the power of words and music to spellbind their listeners," as the authors Philip Carr-Gomm and Richard Heygate write in "The Book of English Magic." Their schooling lasted longer than twelve years and, in the end, they had to know 120 orations and 350 complete stories by heart. What a task. But the most important thing is that they were druids obliged to pass on the old stories so that they would serve the higher good of their tribe. They were preservers of tradition and of the old wisdom, and with their stories they were responsible for the people's inner health. Thus, it never was a mere reciting for pleasure only, for the stories served as a teaching. Oh, and the druids were not just male, the further back I went in history, the more evidence was to be found that in prehistoric times their forerunners, the shamans, were women.

Finding Confirmation at the Museum

My next trip was going to be to the historical museum, where Celtic treasures from several archaeological digs around Berne were displayed. Celtic tribes had been living in this area from about 600 BCE. There is evidence of a growing elite until their integration into the Roman Empire by the end of the first century CE, an elite who took a liking to gold jewelry, precious trading goods, and ceremonial wagons for burial rituals.[25] Obviously, young Celtic girls were not much different from today's girls. They dreamed of jewelry and riches and wanted to marry a prince, no matter whether the year was 2500 BCE or 2013 CE.

The museum's Celtic treasure collection was in a dimly lit room. Brightly lit vitrines displayed the archaeological findings and made the gold and colorful beads they contained sparkle. "Mommy look how beautiful. I would love to have one of those," my daughter exclaimed, standing in front of a vitrine with glass jewelry. She was pointing at bracelets, beads, and rings in bright blue, yellow, and red. Weren't these the colors the ballad mentioned?

To the fountain's basin she pointed,
Which gleamed from among the bushes,
And with blue and yellow and crimson,
The wood's green it painted.

The exhibition notes gave a further explanation: *glass* jewelry and beads were *the* trendy thing during the given Celtic epoch, indeed, they

25 Catalogue of the exhibition "Celtic Treasures," Historisches Museum Bern, 1999

were the ultimate must-haves. So, this was the explanation, why the fountain in the woods near the Celtic settlement bore the name "Glass Fountain." But in the medieval troubadour's understanding, the must-haves of *his* time were gemstones. If he wanted to get his point across in the ballad, he had to speak of *gemstones* and not of *glass* beads.

There was another detail which I had not considered important before, but it fit perfectly now, too. The ballad also speaks of golden braces holding the "gemstones" of the fountain in place, and I could now see golden braces sparkling under the light of the vitrines.

Now I had my answer as to why the plain fountain in the wood was called by the beautiful name of the "Glass Fountain." *The fountain could have once been a basin created with colorful glass beads held together by golden braces!* The ballads and tales still knew about this and passed the knowledge on, though the context had gotten lost over time.

In my article I concluded that there must have once lived a Celtic girl, where nowadays a large recreational wood lies right next to a city. She dreamed of riches, or at least of a man who could abundantly provide her with trendy things. This girl could have been featured in one of today's TV shows. Although there seems to be one big difference. While nowadays to strive for such things is promoted to drive the economy, at the time of the Celtic girl such greed was to be punished. The tale made it clear that it was wrong to only want status and riches. It was *the true heart's values* that counted, and it was such values that at first brought on the generosity of a fairy.

Criticism

Something unexpected happened after this article. It brought me criticism from within my own ranks. My articles had been generally well-received by the public, with quite some praise that got me a teaching position at the Open University. Yet this new perspective of interpreting fairy tales increasingly displeased the storytelling guild, which funded the articles. Since they also sponsored the articles in the hip travel magazine as well, my future collaboration was in jeopardy all along the line. It was believed that I was destroying the *magic* in fairy tales. The more I was able to anchor a tale in a historical time and place, the more my critics said I would take away the tales' enchantment. Was this the case? Was I so selfish as to deconstruct a tale's magic just for the sake of satisfying my curiosity and drawing up connections where there were none to be had? I felt torn. Why not leave it at that, for the tales already offered a large palette of beneficial psychological effects on listeners and readers. *But,* I could sense that there was more to them, and if I just kept digging deeper, I might be able to find even more value and even more concrete relevance for our modern lives.

My storytelling peers argued that the good effect was going to be lost if I proceeded further down the path of demystification. I knew, Joseph Campbell confirmed this concern, when he said that myths ceased to work in the Age of Enlightenment once they were taken too literally.

I had gotten myself into an old philosophical debate between two camps and I was balancing on the fence between them. There were the skeptics, who saw the tradition of fairy tales as teachings of universal truths in symbolic images, mixed with the supernatural, but not connected to concrete historical data. They perceived a gap which on principle cannot be closed. This is the tradition I had been taught in. On the other side, there was the philosophical camp of the positivists, who expected at the core of the myths an historical record. For them the occurrence of a story happened in a contemporary belief system with images and descriptions of a temporal sequence.

I needed to decide on which side of the fence I was going to proceed. Was one camp right and the other wrong? *But* what if both views were valid? What if I looked at tales in a combined way? I couldn't help but think that if a mythological story ceases to work when looked at too *rationally*, it must work the other way around, too. Tales contain universal teaching including a mysterious gap-element, the supernatural, *and* at the same time, they could still be a record of historical facts. This then would mean that I would have to mentally take on the stance and walk in the shoes of our ancestors, who created the stories. They seemed to have experienced a world where the supernatural was included in their day-to-day life. Obviously, to them nature was populated with supernatural entities, and enchantment and disenchantment belonged to their reality. To them, magic must have been what driving cars is to us nowadays: we know how to do it and integrate it easily into our daily lives. Therefore, I figured that a closer look might reveal some prehistoric attitudes that might seem magical to us but was normal to them.

The rebel in me decided to continue my path, keeping both philosophical camps in mind, even if it meant that I lost back-up and the opportunity to publish articles in the name of the storytellers' guild. I was unwilling to view the fairy tales merely as carriers of symbolical images any longer, not after I had found such interesting layers underneath them. The above version of the tale that was collected and edited by Otto Sutermeister in my eyes was a bit bland in comparison to the ballad. Sutermeister must have thought this to be more suitable for his "Children and Household Tales from Switzerland," published in 1869. It featured no personal appearance of the fairy at all. However, should the existence of the medieval ballad, on which Sutermeister based his tale, get unmentioned? If a tale could be restored like a painting by finding a deeper level of it in the old archives and its information corresponded to archeological findings, I regarded it as my duty to bring it forth and see where it would take me.

This was dangerous territory, though, as it seemed to call adversary forces to the scene. Underneath the tales there was something frightening for us modern people, something pre-Christian, pagan, and shamanic, where God is suddenly a *she* and we get exposed to powerful creative forces that shape the world and our destiny.

Chapter 7

Is She a Fairy or a Witch?

"It is our choices, Harry, that show what we truly are, far more than our abilities."
J.K. Rowling

I was relieved to no longer have to be careful about what I was researching and writing about in my articles, especially since I was intrigued by the archaic and pagan material that came to light. So, who was this Celtic fairy flying a dragon chariot accompanied by thunder and lightning? Research for my articles showed that fairy tales often could be taken as accounts of real occurrences. Yet, the aspect of the supernatural was always present as well. That part could not be so easily explained. It was evident that the tales handled the magical as if it were simply a natural thing. A fairy flying with her dragon chariot was nothing to be astonished about. Well, it might be something to be feared after a misstep, like the Celtic maiden's expression of greed, but it was not much different from people in other epochs expecting God's punishment after a wrongdoing.

Celts did not believe in a single, male god. They believed in many gods, a thing we know thanks to their conquerors, the Romans. Since the Celts only kept their folklore in oral form, it was the Romans who reported what kind of culture they had encountered on their campaigns. They translated what they saw into their own cultural expressions. No wonder, when searching for a goddess with a dragon chariot, all I found was a correlation to the Latin Earth goddess *Ceres*, who gave her pupil *Celeus* a dragon chariot to drive around the world to promote farming. Other Earth goddesses, such as the Northern *Freja*, were also said to drive over the land in a chariot to bring fertility, even though I could not find that it was a dragon chariot. So, the goddess in the dragon chariot brings good fate by making crops grow and thus sustaining people with food. Therefore, she is also the one who creates splendors near wells and in gardens—in fact, to all of nature. By bringing beauty and sustenance or, on the other hand, death and destruction onto the material plane, she is also the creator of people's fate.

This led me to believe that the fairy in "The Glass Fountain" was a goddess. Obviously, she appeared from the otherworld to create and to intervene in people's fate. First, her intervention was to the benefit of the young maiden, but then it was to excessively punish her. So, the fairy in the dragon chariot sounded much like one of the goddesses of fate, called by the Romans *Parcae*, by the Greeks *Moires*, and by the Teutons *Norns*.

Mother Holle

If a fairy is equivalent to the goddess of Earth in mythology, then it becomes clear why she appears in the role of a motherly figure, providing her children with the Earth's bounty, but also interfering when things need to be corrected. Nérine was one of many fairies who looked after the shepherds in the Swiss mountains. If they were on good terms with the local fairies, they and their cattle were protected. There was an appreciative relationship between humans and fairies, which was not to be toyed with or else their fate would change for the worse.

Such a mother goddess was also Mother Holle, the Earth goddess of my German-speaking ancestors. In Europe, many folk stories tell of her workings, as we have seen earlier. All of nature's blessings were attributed to her: the renewal in springtime, the growth and blossoming of crops, and its fruits at harvest time in fall. Winter was the time of regeneration. It was her as the grand fairy and her fairy helpers who directed the sap back into the roots, covering all with a protective layer of snow. Around the time of the winter solstice, when the Sun's energy was returning, she reawakened the sap in the trees, as the above tale "Mother Hulda blesses the Earth" conveys.

While I had always been fascinated by Mother Holle as a child, I was also afraid of her. Secretly, I wanted to identify with Golden Mary who was showered with gold after her time at Mother Holle's house. However, believing my mother, I'd much more likely be punished like her stepsister Pitch Mary[26]. I knew I certainly did not deserve gold, for I was far from tidy, even lazier, and certainly too selfish. So better to not even toy with the idea of deserving gold.

From what I know now, the message of the tale is by no means as clear as mothers might want to interpret it, that is, as a warning to get their daughters to clean up their rooms. The German researcher of matriarchy, Heide Göttner-Abendroth, illuminates fairy tales from an

26 The names of the girls in the Grimm tale "Mother Holle" were originally translated with "Pitch Mary" and "Golden Mary." Since they are closer to the German names "Pechmarie" and "Goldmarie," I will use these names, but that they stand for "Dirty Girl" and "Golden Girl."

entirely different angle. She explains that they speak of a social system vastly different from ours today, from a time where all was believed to come from a mother goddess, like Mother Holle. She was the creator of all things, the primordial mother, and humans needed to understand her ways to partner with the goddess. The goddess was believed to live in the otherworld from where she relentlessly created all things on the material plane, yet she needed her creatures on Earth to know the laws and cycles of nature for all to be sustained and live in harmony. The goddess' home was the otherworld, from where she formed the material world, therefore she was mostly invisible, but her work could be seen in her creations. The fairy tales report of this activity and of the interaction between the goddess and the material plane, between the "intelligent spirit," to use Max Planck's term, and our physical world. Göttner-Abendroth explains that while the goddess's nature was eternal, as she was the ruler of cosmos and Earth, a human being was her perishable "hero-self," moving within her creation from birth to death and rebirth.

It becomes clear then that fairy tales model meetings between humans and the supernatural, be it called the goddess or given some other name representing the divine. *Humans are thus taught how they need to deal with the supernatural, the divine, the intelligent spirit behind all of creation.*

Since by nature humans do not remember their mythical origin, the tales help to remind them that they *are* the children of the divine creative force and that they, too, were born out of her otherworldly "womb." The tangible world people live in is the world she created. But it is not a creation which was set up once and for all, but rather it is still continually being created. The human can interact with the divine and the otherworld and even participate in the eternal process of creation.

So, if Mother Holle was the goddess in the otherworld setting the stage for our tangible world, then a girl like Golden Mary was not so much rewarded for being a diligent and obedient little girl by cleaning up her room, but rather was rewarded for helping her in creating reality on Earth. In contrast to her stepsister, who ended up as Pitch Mary, she was attentive and responsive to her surroundings. When she came across a beautiful meadow in Mother Holle's otherworldly realm, she heard that the baked bread was calling out to her and was acting on it. The same happened with the ripe apples on the apple tree. However, Pitch Mary acted entirely different in the same situation—she did not want to burn herself or make herself dirty.

Obviously, it is a skill of a successful heroine to not only hear what things like bread and apples say, but also to act on what they hear, even though it could be to one's disadvantage. So, Mary must perceive the bread's and the apples' needs and must be willing to do something about it. This implies that she has a feel for the things as well as for the right timing. She therefore must be aligned with the seasons and the cosmic creation cycles. In the house of Mother Holle then, another skill is waiting to be learned: the girls need to shake out the bed properly. If we think that here just the skill of a good housewife is required, we interpret the situation wrong. Let's remember that the girls are in the otherworld and Mother Holle is a mother goddess, relentlessly creating the tangible world. If she gets a visitor, it is about something much more profound than daily chores. Instead, the visit is about entering the room of potential, where *creation* is being made.

Good Fairy Godmother or Evil Witch

Interestingly, the looks of Mother Holle as described in the tale are by no means grandmotherly. Rather Golden Mary is frightened at first.

At last she came to a little house, out of which an old woman peeped. But she had such large teeth that the girl was frightened and was about to run away.

Mother Holle has large, scary teeth, a feature prominent also in other fairy tale goddesses, such as the Russian Baba Yaga. With such looks, the mother goddess is no longer called fairy or goddess, but witch. This must depend on one's point of view, mustn't it? The Celtic maiden and Pitch Mary most certainly would have called her an evil witch, while for Golden Mary she was a good fairy.

So Golden Mary is frightened at first, while Pitch Mary, who already heard everything about her from Golden Mary's earlier descriptions, does not show herself much impressed by this powerful entity. Well, she should not have a dismissive attitude toward the divine, not because the divine needs worshiping, but rather regarding the responsibility she gets entrusted with. She gets to make snow down on Earth. She gets to participate in creating the world!

So, what a relief for somebody like me who doesn't like household chores very much, the tale is not about keeping an old witch's house clean. It is about creating the world by means of weather-making. If I could make snow by shaking out the duvet until the feathers fly, believe me, I would do this in a much more cheerful manner. But joking aside, everybody who lives close to nature knows that basic sustenance depends on the weather. Snow and frost at the wrong time can ruin the harvest, a single night of icy temperatures can kill an entire crop, yet, no precipitation at all might result in the catastrophe of a drought. The skill which is being asked for here is not about diligence or laziness, but about discernment. Having the right feel for the cycle's needs is what is required. It is dangerously careless to leave the daily bread in the oven, when it has finished baking, or not to free an apple tree from its heavy burden of ripe fruit. Such an ignorant person in charge of creation is doing more harm than good and ultimately reaps what she sows.

So, this tale is about the attitude it takes to keep the world in harmony. It demonstrates that a respectful inner bearing is a prerequisite for nourishing and taking care of nature. The natural cycles stand above personal desires and need to be considered at all times—or else the consequences are dire. If bread does not get taken out of the oven and the tree is not freed of its apples it is to the peril of the humans who are trying to survive. Those who behave like Pitch Mary do not consider the natural growth cycles and expose themselves to the danger of starvation. Barren land and hunger might be the consequences.

While in the eyes of Golden Mary, Mother Holle is a benevolent mother goddess. In the eyes of Pitch Mary, she is nothing but a mean witch. However, the tale does not pass judgment, but seems to just state things as they are, or as Marita Lück writes in "Zauberkreis der Feen" (Magical Fairy Circle), fairies often represent an "as-well-as" position. So, it just depends on the point of view, whether we see a fairy as a good fairy godmother or an evil witch.

The idea of the benevolent fairy or a good fairy godmother delighted the European storytellers, beginning with the Italian Renaissance continuing through the French baroque era and up until the German romantic period. They took the old story material, just like the medieval bard had done with "The Glass Fountain" and gave the fairy goddess a makeover. She was depicted as a threefold principle, like the goddess of fate, where one of her representations was the *young maiden* (new life), one was the *mother* (middle of life), and one the *old wise woman* (end of life). The old woman represented decay and was also called the crone or the hag. Interestingly, the German term "Hexe" comes from the word "hagazussa," which means somebody who sits on a fence, and with one eye she perceives the material world, and with the other she sees into the otherworld. Therefore, she often is portrayed with one eye only. She is the old person with one foot in this world and with the other already in the other.

The Witch out of Hansel and Gretel

One of the scariest witches of the fairy tale world is the witch in "Hansel and Gretel." When I tell this story to my audiences, the little ones move closer to their parents and hold their hands tightly. They look at me intently and the storytelling situation must be one of coziness and trust, the happy ending always in sight, to create the necessary safe environment to get in touch with the frightening. And the witch is indeed frightening, so calling her a fairy in the sense of a lovely fairy godmother, as found in many French tales, would not be appropriate.

In "Hansel and Gretel," the children must deal with a hag, who is the goddess in her death-bringing aspect. First, she feeds them with gingerbread, which is very nice of her, because otherwise, these kids would have died from hunger even before they had a chance to live. They were born into a world where their own mother could not nourish them and was disconnected from nature's horn of plenty. Something is terribly unbalanced here, there seems to be a trauma at the root of the parents' acting. Their behavior is not normal and might have to do with them being traumatized by war or some kind of bonded labor, as often was the case for farmers in history. But we don't know how this situation came about, we just know where it led to. Two children end up alone in the woods, left to starve. They come into the realm of a witch, the hag aspect of the goddess, who administers life and death. First, she lets them have gingerbread and sweets, then she takes them in and feeds them some more and puts them into warm and cozy beds. For the children to survive, they need to be fed first as an immediate survival measure. They are now in the land between life and death. So, as her first action, the goddess—disguised as a white bird—guides the children into her realm, where food is plenty and they can recover. Then they are taken captive. Gretel must do service for her, maybe like Golden Mary, we don't know, and Hansel is nourished back to strength in a cage.

To be in the old hag's hands, *the goddess of death and decay*, is growing more dangerous from day-to-day. Eventually she—or death—will consume them, if they do not escape or overcome her pull. In many tales, the old witch is performing a milling action, which means that she is churning *the mill of life and death*, sucking everything into her renewing cycle of death and rebirth.

The tale illustrates the children's fight over life and death after being famished so badly. They enter the realm between this world and the other, the realm of the fence, the hag's place, and it is up to them to either marshal all their strengths and jump onto the side of *life*, or to enter the land of *death*. By choosing life and overcoming the witch, they found their innate power and accessed the web of dreams again, where people are connected to the goddess's horn of plenty. Through their experience, they have understood the principle of life and death, which is the principle of Mother Nature's relentless renewing activity. *"Through such observations, the witness bears testimony to immortality and is able to say that we exist beyond space and time, now and forever,"* the Celtic healer Adam tells his disciple.[27]

It can be concluded that the hag's intention was to challenge the children to make a decision. Did they want to live or die? Both options were okay, if they chose to be consumed by death, they would be renewed in the otherworld. However, the witch's action was kind of a shock therapy to jolt their survival instinct.

One thing these tales have in common is that they all contain this message: it is all about choices. How does Mary choose to react when the bread and apples call out to her? Do Hansel and Gretel choose to live or to die? How does the young Celtic maiden react to the riches and beauty she so abundantly receives? What is Hans making out of his ability to understand the animal language? How does the greedy farmer react when he still has an excess of potatoes while his neighbors starve? It seems these tales model an active way of dealing with what is perceived in the environment. The protagonists have a great deal of compassion, but they need to choose to also act on it, make something out of it, only then do they come into the zone, where they can collaborate with the goddess of fate. They decide with their hearts without knowing all the details and consequences in advance, but they let their intuition guide them.

---

27 "Walking with the Sin Eater, A Celtic Pilgrimage on the Dragon Path," Ross Heaven, Llewellyn, 2010, p.60

Chapter 8

Three Wishes Granted

"Yesterday I was clever, so I wanted to change the world,
today I am wise, so I am changing myself."
Rumi

The sad fate of Hansel and Gretel got me thinking about children of the Earth being so unrightfully cut off from their sustaining mother, Mother Nature. Personally, I, too, had felt cut off at one time.

This was in the year right before I found my elixir, the treasure chest full of folklore. Back then, I felt I had no choices and I wished badly for a good fairy godmother, one who granted wishes. Generally, I did not feel supported by the world around me. Sure, I had maneuvered myself into all these situations *but* still, I felt I had a right to have some wishes granted. After all I was trying hard to be a good person and I was struggling to keep my costs down and pay back my debts. My husband tried hard to cheer me up and modeled how to make the best of it by being inventive. He regularly recited our blessings to me. For vacation, we could no longer afford anything other than low-cost camping by a nearby river and the summers, we spent at a very inexpensive, yet absolutely gorgeous spot right by the waterfront. However, I could not enjoy it because I hated the fact that this was not by choice. Our dog's barking at everything and everybody seemed to express my inner state. My husband would not allow me to play the victim, though, and reminded me that this *was* by choice because we could still sit at home. But, I preferred to be angry and depressed. I remember sitting by the river that summer, pen and paper in hand, trying to find a connection to the higher power which I knew dwelled in these beautiful surroundings. But as much as I tried to find the flow, not even the river in front of me could help. I felt as disconnected to this beautiful landscape as could be. I wanted a gift, an insight, the bliss I had lost. I wanted it all and I wanted it right then and there; ideally from a good fairy that would grant me some wishes. Yes, at least three wishes it should be. Had I known then that I was walking through life like Pitch Mary I might have tried to change my attitude. In hindsight, lucky me that I did not meet a fairy back then, I terribly would have wasted my wishes, probably just as the people in this funny English tale:

The Three Wishes

Once upon a time, and be sure 'twas a long time ago, there lived a poor woodman in a great forest, and every day of his life he went out to fell timber. So, one day he started out, and the goodwife filled his wallet and slung his bottle on his back, that he might have meat and drink in the forest. He had marked out a huge old oak, which, thought he, would furnish many and many a good plank. And when he was come to it, he took his axe in his hand and swung it round his head as though he were minded to fell the tree at one stroke. But he hadn't given one blow, when what should he hear but the pitifullest entreating, and there stood before him a fairy who prayed and beseeched him to spare the tree. He was dazed, as you may fancy, with wonderment and affright, and he couldn't open his mouth to utter a word. But he found his tongue at last, and, "Well," said he, "I'll e'en do as thou wishest."

"You've done better for yourself than you know," answered the fairy, "and to show I'm not ungrateful, I'll grant you your next three wishes, be they what they may." And therewith the fairy was no more to be seen, and the woodman slung his wallet over his shoulder and his bottle at his side, and off he started home.

But the way was long, and the poor man was regularly dazed with the wonderful thing that had befallen him, and when he got home there was nothing in his noddle but the wish to sit down and rest. Maybe, too, 'twas a trick of the fairy's. Who can tell? Anyhow down he sat by the blazing fire, and as he sat he waxed hungry, though it was a long way off supper-time yet.

"Hasn't thou naught for supper, dame?" said he to his wife.

"Nay, not for a couple of hours yet," said she. "Ah!" groaned the woodman, "I wish I'd a good link of black pudding here before me."

No sooner had he said the word, when clatter, clatter, rustle, rustle, what should come down the chimney but a link of the finest black pudding the heart of man could wish for.

If the woodman stared, the goodwife stared three times as much. "What's all this?" says she.

Then all the morning's work came back to the woodman, and he told his tale right out, from beginning to end, and as he told it the goodwife glowered and glowered, and when he had made an end of it she burst out,

"Thou bee'st but a fool, Jan, thou bee'st but a fool; and I wish the pudding were at thy nose, I do indeed."

And before you could say Jack Robinson, there the good man sat, and his nose was the longer for a noble link of black pudding.

He gave a pull, but it stuck, and she gave a pull, but it stuck, and they both pulled till they had nigh pulled the nose off, but it stuck and stuck.

"What's to be done now?" said he.

"'Tisn't so very unsightly," said she, looking hard at him.

Then the woodman saw that if he wished, he must need wish in a hurry; and wish he did, that the black pudding might come off his nose. Well! there it lay in a dish on the table, and if the good man and good wife didn't ride in a golden coach, or dress in silk and satin, why they had at least as fine a black pudding for their supper as the heart of man could desire.

It is certainly no piece of cake to wisely use three wishes at one's disposal. This tale motif exists in many different variations in Europe and seems to address the silliness we all could fall prey to by having wishes granted.

The man and his wife were not exactly in the right place to use their wishes wisely. They were driven by feelings of the spur of the moment. Even though the man first did see the fairy and acted according to her wishes, he had to learn the hard way. Desires need to be controlled. If things should materialize from the intangible world into our tangible world, then one would better know exactly what would be wise to wish for. Well, we could argue that he had what he wanted exactly at that moment: a delicious sausage. But then how smart is it to wish for a sausage, when you could have pigs or an entire a farm instead, to make your own sausage? His common sense was overruled by his spur of the moment appetite for black pudding.

In this matter, his wife is thinking on a much larger scale, immediately grasping all the possibilities inherent in three wishes. But she did not do much better. She, too, did not have her impulses under control and was taken over by her spur-of-the-moment anger, which ruined it all and wreaked havoc. Wishing without awareness leads to such results, because it wastes valuable assets. At least in the tale the two are reconciled in the end, sharing and appreciating something they did not have before.

In his book "Selbststeuerung" (self-regulation) the neurobiologist and psychotherapist Joachim Bauer of the University of Freiburg, Germany, writes that habits and reaction patterns are ingrained in the networks of our brains. Self-regulation is a learning process and requires much practice. Neurologically, impulses need to be reconnected for their control. The ability to shut oneself off to temptations and outer stimuli, which only serve a spur of the moment satisfaction, often need to be relearned. It therefore takes training to become consciously able to hold back in favor of more long-term and worthwhile gains. Who can restrain themselves in the short run will gain freedom and reach bigger and more rewarding goals in the long run. Who can think first and anticipate consequences will be better off than who takes hasty actions on a whim. In the end, it is a worthwhile process, because it expands the range of action and thus is something that is highly beneficial for inner balance.

This is what I had to learn. I had to learn to hold back on whims, anticipate consequences, and begin to work on long-term goals. It took me quite some time to shift my awareness back to counting my blessings. By appreciating what I had and give relationships and material matter a new meaning, I came back into alignment with nature and eventually I felt happy, sustained, and nourished again. If I was honest, no amount of money could have solved my problem back then, because it was not the money that was the problem. I had to learn to control my desires and think more long-term by getting aligned with the cosmic timing. I had to finally apply leadership qualities to my own life and give up my victim mentality. This is probably what Adam, the Celtic healer, meant when he said that the web of lies would leave us hanging, while it was the web of dreams that took us home. I had been afraid to own my personal power, which caused the blockages in the first place. I would rather just pout and act on impulses, when instead, I needed to see where my power was. However, this would have asked for a basic trust, faith in a *primordial source* or in *a cosmic order*. It was something I didn't have at the time due to remnants of rather twisted family patterns. I should have had the basic trust of *Hans in Luck*, the famous hero of a Grimm story.

The Basic Trust of Hans in Luck

To people seeing their lives as being in the hands of Mother Nature, the value of things is perceived very differently. Who moves around a great deal and who shares everything he has, amassing possessions makes no sense, unless those things are useful in the moment. Such people trust that Mother Nature will provide them with the right thing at the right time. When this happens, they are grateful and consider themselves lucky, just like Hans in Luck. This tale cheerfully illustrates an alternative model to our taxing things in modern time and age. For Hans, owning things was taxed much differently.

Hans was a young man who had served his master for seven years and received in return *a piece of gold as big as his head.* He intended to go home now to his mother's, but when he had stumbled down the road for a while, he saw a man with a horse. He imagined how nice it would be to sit on that horse, *as if sitting on a chair*, instead of having to carry his heavy load. The rider suggests an exchange, so Hans trades in his gold lump for the horse. *Hans was heartily delighted as he sat upon the horse and rode away so bold and free.*

Now this really goes against our common sense, doesn't it? Trading in a piece of gold as big as his head against only a horse. He must have been cheated, but why then did he feel so delighted after the trade? If the tale would speak of Hans having to carry a lump of lead, would we understand better why Hans was so relieved to trade it? Especially a horse to sit on like on a chair and still move ahead seems appealing, as opposed to walking on foot carrying a lump of gold.

The tale continues that Hans fell off the horse. He said to the man with the cow who came along: *"It is a poor joke, this riding, especially when one gets hold of a mare like this that kicks and throws one off, so that one has a chance of breaking one's neck. Never again will I mount it. Now I like your cow, for one can walk quietly behind her, and have milk, butter and cheese every day without fail. What would I not give to have such a cow."* They traded the horse for the cow. *Hans drove his cow quietly before him and thought over his lucky bargain. "If only I have a morsel of bread—and that can hardly fail me—I can eat butter and cheese with it as often as I like. If I am thirsty, I can milk my cow and drink the milk. My goodness, what more can I want?"*

So, this was what my economics teacher back in my school days meant, when claiming: *Of what use is something for you, if it cannot be eaten, when you are hungry?* Thus, for Hans a cow is better than a horse in that moment, because she gives milk.

The tale continues in this way. Hans traded something in for what seemed to be of lesser monetary value, but still every time, Hans was delighted over the trade. Oh, there were moments when things did not go as he had wished for, like when the cow did not give a drop of milk but rather kicked him, when he tried to milk her. But every time his fate changed for the better—at least from his perspective—and somebody came along and offered him a solution to his problem. The butcher took his stubborn cow and gave him a pig instead, which gave Hans anticipation for a good sausage.

Over time it becomes clear to the listener that in this tale things are being measured with a different yardstick. Every time Hans feels he has just been either saved from a dire fate or he envisions a better future for himself, money-wise, his reality would look like things were getting worse and worse. From pig to goose to grinding stone, but for Hans every new trade is a new opportunity. Even though he is being tricked, it is not so in his eyes. In his eyes he is always sustained by receiving exactly what he wishes for at the exact moment. When he carries two grinding stones with him he feels secure, because it was promised to him that with these he would always be having money in his pocket. *Hans loaded himself with the stones, and went on with a contented heart, his eyes shining with joy. "I must have been born under a lucky star," he cried, "for everything I want happens to me just as if I were a Sunday-child."*

At the end of the story, the stones roll into a well, when he carefully laid them down to have a sip of water. *When Hans saw them with his own eyes sinking to the bottom, he jumped for joy, and then knelt down, and with tears in his eyes thanked God for having shown him this favor also, and delivered him in so good a way, and without his having any need to reproach himself for those heavy stones which had been the only things that troubled him. "There is no man under the sun so fortunate as I," he cried out. With a light heart and free from every burden, he now ran on until he was with his mother at home.*

Today, we view this tale completely differently. We think Hans is a fool and does not notice how much he got cheated. However, he does not think so at all. He gets to experience different adventures during his journey and he always sees the most promising potential in it. Whether he makes the most out of it or not does not matter; for what counts is that he is happy. Hans always goes through life with a content heart.

We modern people however, tax everything from morning till evening. In today's world everything has a price and we constantly must watch out that we receive our money's worth in exchange, or maybe even trick the other person so that the bargain leans toward our side. But doesn't the value of a thing depend on the quality and the circumstances of the moment? Again, my economics teacher's words come to mind: "When sitting alone in the Arctic, naked, cold, and hungry, will a huge pile of gold coins help you survive? Probably not. It does not wrap you, it does not warm you, it does not feed you." Right he was. Wouldn't it be better to be provided with what you really need and when you need it? That would mean true value, wouldn't it?

So, the tale, next to getting us to reflect on the value of things, also shares the wisdom of how to go through a life in the material realm from a matriarchal perspective. Hans' journey home to his mother is his journey to his Great Mother, *the primordial mother*, and ultimately signifies his journey through life. Whatever Hans wishes for comes his way. What a lucky fellow indeed. No matter whether he wishes with intent or only recognizes his blessings in retrospect, he gets what he needs and when he needs it before he gets relieved altogether of the heavy load of the two grinding stones, which symbolize the wheel of time.[28] He now gets released from time and all of the life's material burden and finally gets to return to his *mother*, his creator.

There actually still *was* some hidden fairy action going on during that summer camping by the river. Two months later I was invited to the storytelling event where I found my elixir, and five months later I got a part-time job in bookkeeping.

Thus, over the following years I learned how to responsibly manage money and assets, while at the same time exploring folklore. Finally, I learned to carefully plan, manage well what I already had, and not spend money on a spur-of-the-moment whim. I learned to consciously treasure the tangible things and most of all, the intangible things, such as my beautiful family, our loving relationships, and the rich wisdom in fairy tales, which was there, available and free for all to access. Slowly

28 Mills, grinding stones, or wheels in fairy tales always stand for the cycles of time and their ever-renewing, churning movement. Here, it implies that Hans is now old and tired of life's cycles.

but surely, I adopted their set of values and things started to improve for me. Eventually things got balanced out, of course with the necessary effort on my part. Therefore, I can say it was the fairy tales (and book-keeping) which helped me get back into alignment with Mother Nature's sustaining grace.

Funny enough, our camping trips to the little river are among our family's most cherished memories now, and both our daughters still speak fondly of the adventures climbing rocks in the steep woods of the canyon which separates Switzerland from France. Now I know we were deeply touched by the magic of this relatively untamed nature. I came to realize that my bliss did not depend on repeating six-months-trips in a camper, nor on the balance of my bank account, but rather it came from an appreciative approach to life, acknowledging and embracing what life offered me at any given moment, kind of like *Hans in Luck*.

Chapter 9

Indigenous Roots

"Our crisis is to not be aware of our indigenous roots."
Robin Heath

Experts in the field have long speculated that folk tales contain information on the social organizations and belief systems of our European ancestors. What anthropologists find in prehistoric times are predominantly matriarchal values. They ensure that nature's life-sustaining assets are distributed in a just way to ensure everybody's survival. In the eyes of the creators of our folk tales, planning and managing assets were essential skills to ensure the survival of their communities.

When Mother Nature's assets are not handled well, there eventually will be no food left in wintertime. And winter comes. Always. For all to be nurtured and taken care of, a tribe had to ensure that personal leadership was being taught and understood by all members.

Sharing, especially food-sharing, was one of the most important values and secured the survival of all. In contrast, instant gratification on a spur-of-the-moment impulse could endanger an entire tribe. So, rules like the following could provide the right structure for a society, where all were dependent on others to survive:

1. All stems from the Great Mother, thus all life is related and must be valued equally.
2. Everybody in a clan is considered valuable and contributes with his skills to the well-being of the group.
3. Leadership emerges from wisdom.
4. Therefore, women and men are equal, though it is the women who give birth to new life.
5. Who gives birth to new life must obviously be the surrogate of the Great Mother and therefore needs to be honored and listened to.
6. Life moves in cycles (as opposed to being linear), as seen everywhere in nature, in the seasons and in the stages of human life. Birth, life, death, and then the cycle begins anew. Therefore, there is no death, just transformation.
7. Since food nourishes the clan, it is considered holy and must not be wasted.
8. As women naturally know how to nurture their children, they should also oversee the storage and distribution of food.
9. Every person must be equally fed. If one person is hungry, everybody is hungry.
10. Everything is shared. Collecting possessions is not an issue.

These are values the folk tales build upon, as researchers of myth and matriarchy have found.[29] Matriarchal structures were closely tied to regular daily life. Just like in *Mother Holle*, the goddess is found living in the otherworld while her creatures live in the material world on the other side of the veil. They are living with the flow of the Great Mother's creative energies, the seasons and cycles. On Earth, her creatures are all representatives of the goddess. A bird who is hatching its eggs is contributing to the creation just as much as a snake eating some of them to live and then laying its own eggs. The creative source was seen to manifest and act through its beings and thus also through humans. In the matriarchal worldview there was no split between rites and daily chores, for every single chore must be done in heartfelt connection with Spirit, the creative force behind all things. Folk tales have been found to portray this kind of belief system, where every action is viewed as sacred and the goal is always to be attentive and mindful. They seem to reveal our ancestors' religious approach to life.

A Short Glance at the History of our Ancestors

For many hundreds of thousands of years, people had lived in small groups in Europe, leading a nomadic non-violent life, as archeological evidence shows. They lived in sync with nature and one another. Resources were plentiful, and life was peaceful. There was no obsession with possessions, because everything was there and shared. All life was

29 See "*Die Göttin und ihr Heros*" (The Goddess and her Heroes), Heide Göttner-Abendroth, Kohlhammer, Stuttgart, 2011 and also "Der enteignete Mythos" (The Expropriated Myth) Gerda Weil, Ulrike Helmer Verlag, Königstein, 1996

understood to be benevolent. There did not seem to have been many fights or territorial claims. In fact, archeologists have not found any signs of violence on bones recently discovered in the Dinaledi Chamber, part of the Cradle of Humankind World Heritage Site in South Africa. This probable ancestor of ours from two- to-one-point-five million years ago has been named *Homo naledi*.[30] Even though the archeologists expected signs of violence on the skulls and bones, there were none. *Homo naledi* had placed their dead carefully into a cave, which to them could have well been *the mother's womb*, where figuratively all life is transformed and becomes new again.

According to DNA technology, our direct ancestors can be traced back to 200,000 years ago, when they lived in Africa and a line of their descendants later moved into Europe some 55,000 years ago. Large-breasted female figures of ivory and stone, figures with animal heads, as well as flutes made from the fragile bones of a bird have been found in caves, which are at least 40,000 years old. Our ancestors were not only artistically talented, they must have also performed ceremonies, with singing and dancing, according to the Swedish author and science journalist Karin Bojs.[31]

The changing climate due to cyclic variations in the orbit and tilt of the Earth had a large-scale influence on the face of a landscape and the lives of indigenous peoples. The varying distance of the Earth to the Sun makes summers hotter and winters colder. Over the span of 10,000 years, this results in ages which bind large bodies of water in sheaths of

30 See "Dawn of Humanity" by Graham Townsley, PBS NOVA National Geographic documentary, 2015, https://www.pbs.org/video/nova-dawn-humanity/

31 "My European Family, the First 54,000 Years" by Karin Bojs, Bloomsbury Sigma, London, New York, 2017

ice to the effect that the sea level around a shore drops, adding land to a shoreline, or—in other ages—the ice melts due to higher temperatures and land is covered by water. Depending on the temperature, the landscape and its vegetation changes and the inhabitants need to adapt over time.

After the last Ice Age, about 11,000 years ago, the landscape took on the shape we know today. Archeological findings reveal that about 1,500 years after that, for the first time in history, people started to settle down. They chose an area which has become known as the Fertile Crescent, a moist and fertile half-moon shaped area around the Nile Valley and Nile Delta stretching from Palestine to Turkey, bordering on the Persian Gulf in the south. At the same time, small indigenous tribes of hunters and gatherers were scattered all around Europe. They, too, began to sustain themselves with a less-nomadic lifestyle.

The British archeologist Barry Cunliffe writes that in Megalithic times about 4,500 BCE there were vivid exchange networks all over Europe, where seeds, animals, flints, pebbles, and tools were exchanged. People were trading goods and know-how of various skills. The first gold appeared in the trading networks in the fifth millennium BCE.[32]

As we have seen, the content of our European fairy tales displays historical facts *as well as* symbolical metaphors. Hans in Luck could have lived during a time when matriarchal values started to dissolve and gold gained in importance. Since that tale also features a goose for a christening feast, we could take it to be historically placed at a time when part of the population was already Christian, and part was still pagan. It is an

32 "Europe between the Oceans, 9000 BC – AD 1000," Barry Cunliffe, Yale University Press, New Haven, Connecticut, 2008

interesting little detail in the story which reveals the struggle between the old and the new religion. The goose symbolizes the goddess in the old religion and now she was going to be sacrificed at a christening feast. After the exchange, when Hans walks away with the goose, he says to himself: *"How glad my mother will be."* He saved the mother goddess from being sacrificed for the new, Christian god.

A recent study aimed at tracing the origin of folk tales by using the old Indo-European language combined with methods of biology. Analyzing the cross-cultural distribution of folk tale types in their relationships to spatial, genetic, and linguistic patterns, Sara Graça da Silva, a researcher at New University of Lisbon, and Jamshid J. Tehrani, a Durham University researcher, found, in essence, confirmation in what matriarchal and anthropological research into European folklore had brought to light before: *"We show that these oral traditions probably originated long before the emergence of the literary record,"* Garça and Tehrani report. Narrative motifs included in their study were up to 6,000 years old, the time of the Neolithic people. *"These stories have survived without being written. They have been told since before even English, French, and Italian existed. They were probably told in an extinct Indo-European language."*[33]

So, archaeological findings, anthropological studies on matriarchal societies, plus linguistic studies all start to come to the same conclusion: *The folk tales are our intangible European heritage from a time, when we too lived the lifestyle of an indigenous culture.*

33 rsos.royalsocietypublishing.org/content/3/1/150645

Our Very Own Roots

What a revelation: the folk and fairy tales were thousands of years old and marked our very *roots*. This meant that we too had stories at the base of our culture, just like any other indigenous folk. Of course, we did. Our European history could not have only consisted of invasions, bloody battles, and witch burnings, the things we learned in history class. But why did nobody tell us more about the prehistoric times, the times in history before writing had been invented, the time when Ötzi crossed the Alps and gigantic stone monuments were built along the shore regions all over Europe? Why were those ancestors depicted uniformly as "stone age" people, evoking the image of cavemen, who drug their wives around by the hair?

By now, I knew better. This ancient world showed to be a colorful place, where at first, after the last Ice Age, people in Europe lived in the woodlands or close to the shores in small tribes. They were hunters and gatherers whose worldview came from their close relationship to Mother Nature that sustained them. They made music, danced, and told stories. Their belief system was what today we would call "shamanic."

At the same time, their contemporaries in Anatolia already tested out life as farmers in the Fertile Crescent, which is right to the east of Europe, as we have seen. Not so long before, they too had been hunters and gatherers, but now, the good climate allowed them to stay in one place. Just like the hunter-gatherer tribes over in Europe, the farmers still believed in a kind of early mother-goddess, the German religion scientist Ina Wunn writes. "*This supreme being (Mother Goddess or*

Dema) was obviously known, however, was not an object of cult."[34] She was not seen as a single supernatural entity, but rather as a *natural principle.* She was perceived as being on the inside of everything as well as on the outside. This way of thinking and perceiving the world must have been the very basis of our ancestors' matriarchal values, both in Europe and in Anatolia.

Probably due to climate changes and food scarcity, those first farmers of Anatolia left their early settlements and moved into Europe, where they began to mingle with the local hunter-gatherer tribes, who themselves had started to test out a more sedentary lifestyle. A vivid exchange began to happen, where farming know-how, tools, and all sorts of inventions, such as the wheel, were shared. Plant seeds, domesticated animals like sheep and horses, were traded. At a fast rate, people developed from being nomads to becoming farmers and craftsmen. It was the time of a massive creative change, called the Neolithic Revolution, maybe the biggest change in mankind's history, apart from today's digital revolution.

But in all of this, the supernatural and magical played no lesser role in their lives than it did before, when they lived the nomadic lifestyle. They were still very aware of their connection to the mysterious divine behind the veil and they knew of their dependency on the creative source.

Only now, our settled ancestors had to learn a new way of interacting with Mother Nature. If they wanted to successfully live in only one

34 "Götter, Mütter, Ahnenkult, Religionsentwicklung in der Jungsteinzeit" (Gods, Mothers, Ancestor Worship, Religious Development in the Neolithic Age), Ina Wunn, VML Vlg Marie Leidorf 2001, partially in English, p. 182

place and grow their own food, they had to study her cycles, the weather, and the seasons.

The realization that the fairy tales contained the wisdom teachings of our ancestors, who lived so close to nature that they knew its very laws, was priceless for me. It meant that my notions had guided me in the right direction. I got more than I bargained for. They brought me back to my roots, back to all our European roots. They gave me deep insights and healing. No longer did I need to consult other indigenous cultures' wisdom. Here, I had found a wisdom in images which I could understand, because it was in my very genes. I had not been wrong to rely on the fairy tales for helping me out of my crisis.

So, the European folk and fairy tales were modeling a well-balanced life, in fairness and healthy relationships, with an even give-and-take interaction between all beings on Earth and its creative divine source. These stories were as valuable today as 6,000 years ago. Only I needed to understand their context, but that was not so difficult after all, since the stories spoke a straightforward language from heart to ear, and ear to heart.

Suddenly, I understood that my favorite fairy tale, which my mother had to read to me over and over when I was a child ("The Little Blue Bird") contained the remedy to heal exactly those wounds she inflicted on me. I realized that I had always perceived myself as the heroine of that tale, who tried to free herself from the web of lies set up by an abusive mother, who did everything to avoid her own wounds. I so longed to create a web of dreams instead. So, unconsciously my mother equipped me with a map from problem to solution. Funny enough, the heroine in my favorite tale had to consult the Sun, Moon and stars on her way to happiness , something I also did by studying astrology.

The idea that fairy tales contain signposts that guide people out of a web of lies toward a web of dreams had me pick up my search for a correlation between the hero's journey and cosmic events again.

Part II

A Balanced Sun-Moon Calendar

The Second Message in European Fairy Tales

Chapter 10

The Skills of a Folk Tale Hero

"If I have the belief that I can do it, I shall surely acquire the capacity to do it even if I may not have it at the beginning."
Mahatma Gandhi

To have found our European indigenous roots in the beloved tales of my childhood made me very fortunate. It had been seven years since I first learned about the hero's journey, and even though no screenplay was written, and no alignment was found with cosmic events yet, I still felt that my search had come up with something incredibly valuable: I had found the way back to my indigenous roots. It provided me with teachings that helped me restore balance in life and access bliss again.

This I wanted to share in a book now. Since I was fascinated by the skills of the prehistoric "indigenous" folk tale protagonists, I was going to specifically explore those. They were best demonstrated in the *wonder tales,* also called *magic tales.* The best-known fairy tales fall into this category, like "Cinderella," "Sleeping Beauty," "Mother Holle," and "Hansel and Gretel," to name only a few.

Regardless of their gender, protagonists in fairy tales obviously demonstrated skills that reflected prehistoric *matriarchal* values, other than the heroes of written myths of a later age, which mostly displayed *patriarchal* values.

I began to list the attributes of fairy tale heroes and heroines, since it seemed to be the secret to what opened a whole world to them, a world full of wonder, magic, and unexpected, benevolent support in their fate.

They:

- were intuitive
- were guided by the heart
- were patient
- were hospitable
- were attentive to their surroundings
- were helpful and nurturing
- were protective toward others
- were discerning the important from the unimportant, the good advice from the bad, and thus could not easily be deceived by lies and manipulations
- were generally, not selfish
- knew when to act
- were able to decide
- knew how to act rightly and with integrity
- could recognize help and accept it
- had access to an inner well of creativity
- considered themselves to be free beings
- did not bend to rules which made no sense
- were able to size up their adversaries correctly

- were driven to move forward for a good cause, even if consequences might be dire
- were honest, but knew when it was better to keep quiet
- knew what they were entitled to and when it was appropriate to claim it
- were humble and did not take more than their fair share
- were neither deceived by material gains nor utterly attached to them
- had a feeling and respect for natural timing and laws
- were attuned to synchronicity

This list could go on and on. All attributes came from their virtues of personal integrity and attunement to natural timing. It was mirroring their inner values, expressed in every thought and deed. This seemed to be the true source of their natural acting and allowed them to establish a direct relationship with the invisible destiny-shaping force, spirit, the divine or the then-called *Great Mother*.

Yet with patriarchy on the rise, values and virtues began to shift. Humanity now allowed other behaviors, and strive, deception, manipulation, and power over others became tolerable. Warriors, fighters, and conquerors were celebrated. Consequently, the male folk tale hero began to be called "the simpleton." In a patriarchic society, this kind of hero was now considered weak and stupid and his "feminine" ways were no longer understood.

More so, if the fairy tale protagonists modeled how to succeed in becoming a king or a queen, then this kind of message had to be suppressed. It was *critically dangerous* for the patriarchal world. It needed to be put down, forbidden, ridiculed, or plain called a lie-story, together with *all* feminine attributes. As you might remember, the word "Mär" means message and the ending is a form of belittlement in German. Since the fairy tale protagonists modeled how to act out of integrity, they disabled the patriarchic concept of serfdom. They went against the established systems of bondage and suppression, the artificially constructed web of lies of patriarchy, where only a few received all of nature's bounty, the food, the power, and the riches, while leaving most of the people enslaved and exploited. In history, parallel to the fairy tales, the women and their feminine wisdom got suppressed and discriminated against, especially since it was the women who were physically connected to the natural cycles. Consequently, humanity lost the balance between feminine and masculine attributes over the past millennia.

In the end Freud even attributed an aggression drive to human beings. However, according to the latest research of neurologists and biologists, there is no such thing as Freud's aggression drive, so it is *not* a natural given that we want to harm and suppress one another, yet, we carry in our DNA the traumas of former generations. Those who have been traumatized by wars famines, sexual abuse, torture, flight, or expulsion and do not manage to heal the wounds and balance life out, pass their scars on to the next generation. Without knowing it, the next generation will then act as if they themselves had been exposed to the traumatizing situation, continuing the negative spiral of a sad destiny.[35] They unwillingly contribute to the collective web of lies. I know a lot of people who for this reason decide against having children. They do

35 See "Schmerzgrenze: Vom Ursprung Alltäglicher und Globaler Gewalt" (Pain Barrier: from the Origin of Everyday and Global Violence), Joachim Bauer, Heyne Verlag, 2013

not want to pass on what they suffered. The only way out of this seems to be the path of awareness and healing, eventually finding back into a balance.

Chapter 11

Spinning and Weaving

"Humankind has not woven the web of life. We are but one thread within it. Whatever we do to the web, we do to ourselves. All things are bound together. All things connect."

Chief Seattle

One striking attribute of the exclusively female heroines in European tales was spinning and weaving. At a certain point in the story, they seemed to magically spin themselves a new future. The male heroes on the other hand, were looking for brides who knew best how to spin and weave. Added that the tales were implying that destiny was not set, but could be altered by the protagonists' choices, I started to wonder whether in the wonder tales it was demonstrated how destiny could be woven. While spiders would be the most obvious animal to show up in context of weaving the web of life, in European fairy tales the theme of weaving and spinning is often represented by toads.[36]

36 I only came to truly understand this when I chanced to watch a toad lay her eggs. One day in early spring, I was walking around our little garden pond, when suddenly, I became aware that two toads were sitting on top of each other and one of them was amid laying a long string of eggs. The next day I found the long egg-string carefully hung in the grass by the waterline. It was literally woven into the long blades which bent down into the water. Now I understood. First the toad had been spinning the thread containing her eggs, then she wove the string into the grass and safely placed it on the shoreline. She indeed was a very fine spinner and soon the next generation of toads was going to come forth in our pond. See the Swiss tale "The Three Brothers" as an example of a spinning toad on my website andreahofman.com.

This idea got me thinking, especially since graphic depictions of transiting planets in astrology (*see graphic below*) also seemed to resemble shuttles that were weaving a thread into the round image of a chart.

Wasn't the astrological chart like a round loom and the moving planets like shuttles weaving threads into that loom? In a way, the image was also like a spider's web that was being woven. I knew there were Native American stories about Grandmother Spider weaving *the web of life*. The Anglo-Saxon term for *the web of destiny* was "wyrd," which again was close to the Celtic healer Adam's *web of dreams*.

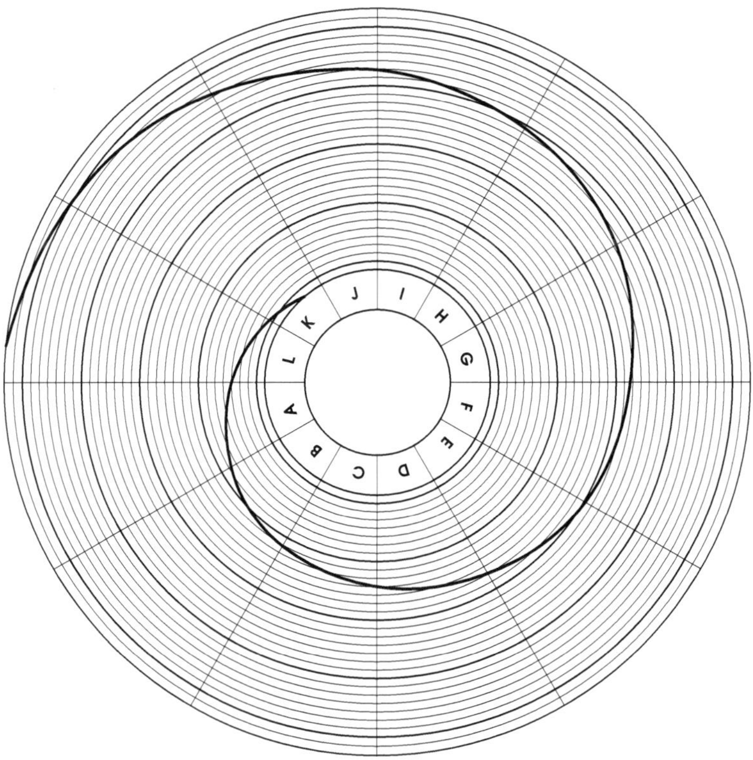

Arachne, the Weaver

The image of the weaving motion began to manifest itself after my encounter with a little spider that bit me on the back one day when I was hiking in the Alps near our home. It was a bright, warm day in springtime, when I laid down in an alpine meadow to take a rest during the hike up. The sunny place right by a little lake must have been perfect for a spider to weave her nest between two stalks of grass, and here I came, an intruder in her realm, and now even laying down on her nest.

Her bite made me jump up and reminded me of another encounter with a spider years before in California. That time it had been a much, much larger spider, a tarantula, which was caught by our neighbors at a campsite. From a safe distance, I stared at the tarantula and felt all the hairs on my body stand up on end. Somehow, I felt connected to that courageous spider, for she did not run away after her careful release, but rather firmly stood her ground, pumping her body up and down. Later I read that she was bombarding us with tiny hairs as a defense mechanism. As I was watching her, I was tingling from head to toe and my every nerve cell seemed to be in a state of consciousness. I have never forgotten my feelings of admiration for that fierce little creature, so this alpine spider mother had my full sympathy as well while defending her nest.

That must have been the *spider power* shamans talk about, which so clearly re-entered my life at this point. I took these two encounters as a hint that it was time to explore this topic and I started to meditate on it. The more I learned about the spider and her energies, the more I noticed that a personal healing was going on. I had been skillfully woven into a mother's spider web, who herself had been so traumatized as a child as to create a sticky net of manipulation for her children. Now, in this "spider-therapy," I was being disentangled from the shadow side of spider energy, as I came to learn.

I became curious about Grandmother Spider's magical lore and found the following Navajo story in a brochure at the Nonam Museum in Zurich.

The Legend of the Loom

A long time ago, Wandering Woman lived with her folk, the Navajo, in a land of deep, red canyons. One winter, when ice-spirit blew his cold breath through the canyons, Wandering Woman had a dream. First, she saw a bird gathering dry twigs and grass, making a nest. Then she dreamt of a caterpillar pupating and a beaver building a dam. Lastly, she saw a spider spinning a web in her dream. When Wandering Woman awoke, she quickly did her daily chores and walked to the canyon. There was smoke rising to the sky on Spider Rock. She climbed the rock and looked down the smoke hole. There was an old woman sitting at a loom. Her face was creased, and her teeth looked like bear claws.

"Who are you? "Wandering Woman asked.

"I am Spider Woman," the old woman answered.

Wandering Woman was curious: "What are you doing?"

"As the bird makes his nest, the caterpillar pupates, the beaver builds a dam, and the spider spins a web, I weave." The old woman patted the ground, inviting her in to sit down next to her.

"I don't fit through the hole," Wandering Woman replied.

Therefore, Spider Woman blew through the hole so that it grew bigger and bigger, until Wandering Woman could enter.

"Will you teach me how to weave?"

"Yes, I will, for that is why I had you come."

Spider Woman asked her husband to build a loom for Wandering Woman, and for four days she taught her how to weave. On the first day, they wove a blanket the color of the abalone shell; on the second day, they wove one of the color of the sky; on the third day a red one like the color of fire; and on the fourth day a black rug like the color of darkness.

Spider Woman said: "Now you are ready," and gave her a new name, Asthlo Asdzaa, the Weaving Woman.

Only the light of the quarter moon was shining when Asthlo Asdzaa returned home. There, she set up her loom and started weaving. Four days and four nights she continued, but when the rug was halfway done, she noticed that she had made mistakes. She removed row after row and re-wove them. Again, she detected a mistake, removed, and re-wove it. Four times this happened, but she just could not get the pattern right. She became very angry and finally tore the rug off the loom and tore it all to pieces. Then she threw it out of her home.

That night she did not sleep well. In her dreams the cotton strings entangled her as if the unfinished rug was pulling her to continue to weave. Early the next morning, Asthlo Asdzaa saw Spider Woman outside. She was sitting at the recovered loom, re-weaving the rug which Asthlo Asdzaa had torn apart the night before. "When you start to weave, your thinking-spirit enters the rug and lives in it from then on. The spirit stays, even if you stop weaving, and it will not let you rest until the rug is finished. Therefore, never give up."

Mother Holle Revisited

Again, it was the goddess of fate who was teaching a girl how destiny got woven.[37] Often in tales a fundamental transformation is accompanied by weaving a new cloth. The symbol of a fabric or the act of spinning or weaving are used to demonstrate how a new reality gets created.

As in Mother Holle, Asthlo Asdzaa meets a scary goddess with "teeth looking like bear claws." Again, the tale of "Mother Holle" adds valuable insights, even though it only marginally mentions the act of spinning. At the beginning, Golden Mary does not lose a shoe or any other old object, but she loses her *shuttle*. With this, the tale informs us that it concerns the matter of spinning and therefore of creating destiny.

Every day the poor girl had to sit by a well, by the side of the road, and spin and spin till her fingers bled.

Blood stands for Mary's life-force, and she was obliged by her mean stepmother to spin so much that her life-force began to drip out of her.

Now it happened that one day the shuttle was marked with her blood, so she dipped it in the well, to wash the mark off, but it dropped out of her hand and fell to the bottom.

So, at the moment the shuttle falls into the well, her life is handed over to the goddess. Asthlo Asdzaa also had to pass through a hole to enter the divine realm. In European folklore, wells have always been considered the dwelling places of fairies, as we know from universal mythology and from "The Glass Fountain." The well is the entrance to the goddess's realm, the otherworld. Does Mother Holle, the goddess

---

37 The goddess of fate was considered spinning the thread of life (birth), measuring its length (lifespan) and cutting it (death). In mythology, the goddess often is portrayed threefold, one for each task, and those three were seen to rule over the past, present, and future.

of fate, know this girl who is sitting there close to the entrance of her realm day after day? Is a girl wasting her life-force by spinning herself a miserable destiny? Does she even mean to invite her and show her how a life thread can be spun which brings forth a better life, just like Asthlo Asdzaa was invited by Grandmother Spider? In any case, "fate" has it that her stepmother makes her jump into the well to go fetch it.

She then fainted. And when she awoke and came to herself again, she was in a lovely meadow where the sun was shining and many thousands of flowers were growing.

While diving down into the well to fetch the shuttle, Mary nearly drowns. She loses consciousness and enters the otherworld in a dream state. It could be a near-death experience, but it could also be a trance-like state known from shamanic journeys. In any case, she gets a glimpse behind the veil of the otherworld, where reality is being "woven." Not only that, she is invited to participate in the process. She gets to do chores, which imply a cyclical activity where she gets to contribute to the seasons on Earth, as we have seen in Chapter 7. A girl, who desperately needs to know how to change her destiny for the better, gets a chance to see how things get created on the material plane.

But just the act of doing something feverishly, like Golden Mary's spinning at the fountain until her fingertips get bloody, does not bring the desired results. Grandmother Spider drew the Navajo girl's attention to the fact that the work must be done with intent, stamina, and the willingness to learn. Combined with careful attention and forward thinking, the act of weaving or spinning can then become an act of *true* creation.

In the "Indian Village of Ahwahnee,"[38] I once learned that the performance of any task, not just the one of weaving, is considered a holy act for exactly this reason. Be it cooking, crafting, gathering berries, or healing with plants, every single task is a communion with the living spirit in the material involved. Every act is considered a meditative, concentrated practice to take something and transform it into something different.

So, when snow is made, Golden Mary learns how to handle the creative energies to bring forth something new, which is going to influence the web of life. Something non-existing is being born into existence. It is a birth. It is sacred. Both girls need therefore to become aware of the *thinking-spirit* when doing a chore. This means that communication with the creative life-shaping force happens and they need to be in a kind of energetic exchange with all that surrounds them and always react to its needs at the right time.

Once communication is started with the life-shaping energies through the act of weaving or spinning, sensitivity for time and matter grows and the heroine can participate in co-creating tangible results. Göttner-Abendroth writes in "The Goddess and her Hero" that the goddess initiates a heroine into becoming her surrogate on the material plane.

Golden Mary certainly had to learn the chores of a goddess when entrusted with making snow. Something was being born from the otherworld into the tangible world. It was an act of creation. For it to turn out for the highest good of everyone involved, Golden Mary's personal integrity and dedication were required. Also, she had to get a feel for

38 A reconstructed village of the Sierra Nevada Miwok in Yosemite National Park, USA

the divine creation energies and come into alignment with their natural flow. This know-how was a prerequisite for her to co-weave her own fate and that of others in the future. She would then be able to produce gold instead of pitch.

Things could quickly get out of hand though, if not held in check by intent and attention. Pitch Mary, to the contrary, was idle, the tale says. She did not spin and had no interest in learning anything about co-weaving her destiny. Ignorant and disinterested in the needs and timings of nature, she believed that bread and apples would land in her mouth without her doing anything about it. Therefore, by consequence, all she would eventually have for to harvest was pitch. Pitch is tar, a black liquid and product from organic materials made through destructive distillation. Thus, Pitch Mary caused destruction and the separation of things with her ignorant behavior. Bread and apples, nature's bounty, went to waste because of her. Her wages were, as the result of her omissions, a viscous liquid sticking to her for all to see.

Wise Leadership

Golden Mary and Asthlo Asdzaa both returned to their lives on the material plane well-equipped and eager to serve as the representatives of the goddess. Now they would spin life in harmony with the divine creative energies, just how they learned from the goddess. Their wages after the apprenticeship were "gold", a set of new tools and talents for all to see and learn from.

The door was opened, and just as the maiden was standing beneath the doorway, a heavy shower of golden rain fell, and all the gold clung to her, so that she was completely covered with it.

Her "gold" is the equivalent to a saint's halo, or a princess's crown. When tales speak of a princess, a queen, a prince, or a king it is this golden halo they imply. A crowned fairy tale protagonist is someone who has been initiated into being the surrogate of the goddess in the material realm.

Many mythological stories speak of "the golden aura" or "golden crown" a person receives when having met the divine. It is a sign that they learned about their mystical origin and were taught how divine creation happened in the ever-turning cycles of nature.

So, fairy tale protagonists who receive the "golden aura" or the "royal crown" in folk tale language are the ones who are attuned to the divine creation process. They are willing to take on a leadership role in their community because they are wise and know life is like a web. They know that all is connected and every action, every thought, has an effect and can be felt by other beings as well. Nobody and nothing can ever be outside of that web of life. It is constantly created in a cyclical motion. Nothing is isolated, because nothing can exist alone.

For the material world, it is essential to have leaders who know about the divine creation process. This needs to be the foundation of their wise leadership. They need to preserve and pass on what has been preserved and passed on for generations: The wisdom how to weave destiny attuned to the creative energies. Then, everybody will be sustained by nature's bounty.

Finishing that "Rug"

Looking at tales from that perspective greatly intrigued me and I somehow felt driven by a *thinking-spirit* just like the Navajo girl, Asthlo Asdzaa. I was still trying to find a connection between the hero's journey and astrology and my wish to finally finish that "rug" was very strong. At one point, the idea of a spider web being woven up in the sky had me take a closer look at the asteroid Arachne. Maybe it was "her" who was secretly weaving the web of life by orbiting our birth charts. I compared her cycles to the hero's journey in wonder tales and my personal diary entries to determine if there could be a match. Unfortunately, there was none. This theory was not working, either. However, imagining a planetary body to be like a shuttle that weaves its thread through a birth chart and comparing its trace to the hero's journey, got me thinking in the right direction.

Chapter 12

A Story in the Sky

"And the seasons they go 'round and 'round
And the painted ponies go up and down
We're captive on the carousel of time.
We can't return we can only look behind,
From where we came
And go round and round and round
In the circle game."

Joni Mitchell

The image of destiny being woven by planetary cycles round and round the astrological chart began to solidify in my mind. If the wonder tales were providing a reliably recurring structure of the heroic journey, as I noticed every time I learned a new tale by heart, and they were stemming from the Neolithic Age, then I would need to find out what Neolithic people knew about astronomy.

I imagined our ancestors standing on a hilltop gazing up into the sky and watching the Sun, Moon, Mercury, Venus, and the other planets circling the Earth.[39] Turning on their own axis, they must have made out

39 In astrology the Sun and the Moon are also referred to as planets, although in scientific terms, they are not.

significant markers on the earthly horizon to tie their planetary observations to a fixed point on Earth. These marked points could be either mountain tops in alpine regions, megalithic rocks in plains, or along the sea shores. [40] The Neolithic people were known to live in those regions and they were also known for building incredible Megalithic monuments, such as Stonehenge, Avebury, Ring of Brodgaror or Callanish, to name only a few in the U.K. It was a widespread phenomenon of that age and there are many Megalithic sites to be found all over Europe.[41]

So, our Megalithic ancestors must have first established an observatory point and marked it with a stone they could sit on. Then they divided the 360-degree horizon around them into segments separated by markers, and then they could comfortably observe the changing skies in relation to the determined fixed points on Earth. As they were sitting there, night after night, year after year, the rhythmic and elegant dance of the Sun and Moon must have become obvious to them. They could well have described it as a weaving motion all around their dwelling point. The Sun and Moon went round and round, rising above their heads and plunging again below the horizon, only to rise again in a slightly different position. *"These two 'Lights' represented the two basic factors in human experience: light and life,"* astrologer Alexander Ruperti writes in "Cycles of Becoming, The planetary pattern of growth."

Perceived from the Earth, the Sun takes its yearly rounds through rising and setting positions. The Moon mirrors the same positions

40 See works of Paul Devereux (f.e. "Symbolic Landscapes," Gothic Image, 1992), Heide Göttner-Abendroth (f.e. "Berggöttinnen der Alpen," (Mountain Goddesses of the Alps) Edition Raetia, 2016, Kurt Derungs, (f.e. "Landschaften der Göttin," (Landscapes of the Goddess) edition amalia, 2000, or Robin Heath ("Temple in the Hills," Bluestone Press, 2016) and many more.

41 Visit megalithic.co.uk for maps of all European countries and their listed Megalithic sites.

within one month. It takes 235 lunar phases over 19 years till they meet again in the same place.[42] The Moon moves thirteen times faster than the Sun. Who carefully watches their cycles over a long period of time might get the impression that *the Moon is weaving its silvery thread into the Sun's golden filament,* an image that is often used in fairy tales.[43]

In any case, Neolithic observers in the northern hemisphere would have remembered over which mark in the landscape the Sun had risen that morning and would have noted it as the east point. Opposite at 180 degrees, they would know that there is the west point, the setting point of the Sun. It must have been also clear to them that north and south would be at the quarter points, or at 90 degrees between those two points. The observers would want to put around them a number of standing stones as markers and then place themselves in the middle of the circle. It certainly helped to have a whole bunch of markers all around them, not one for every single degree in the 360 degrees, since this would make up an entire wall, but a certain number to help divide the circle into segments. Now, they would get to watch the Sun and the Moon rise and set and see them travel along an imaginary band in the sky called the ecliptic. They must have noticed that even though star constellations were scattered in the sky all around them, the Moon, Sun, and planets mostly only travelled along the ecliptic path. It seemed to be somewhat like a road, crossing only certain constellations, which came to be called the zodiac. We know that at one point in history, these

42 This is the so-called Metonic cycle.

43 Many a tale speaks of a special tissue made up of silver and golden threads. One such example is the Swedish tale "The Princess in the Cavern," found in "Svenska folk-sagor och äfventyr" (Swedish folk-fairy tales and adventures), Gunnar Hyltén-Cavallius and George Stevens, Stockholm, 1844 . See fairy tale examples in Part III of this book.

luminaries were thought to be gods and goddesses, who rode their chariots on the band of the ecliptic, round and round the Earth.

Angles or Aspects

I started to wonder whether the Neolithic observers also considered the distance between two planets as we do today. They must have; it is only logical. Why else would they have set markers in the landscape which served as fixed points for observation? Viewed from the Earth, the distance between any two wandering luminaries can be easily measured. We measure them in angles and they might have done the same back then. The degree between the Sun and the Moon constantly varies, since both are constantly in a "dancing" motion at different speeds. In astrology, we call these angles of separation *aspects*, which means "to look at something." Therefore, the aspects serve to describe the relationship between two planets. The Sun and the Moon look at each other, just like dancing partners. Viewed from the Earth, they seemingly "meet" for a short moment, the moment of conjunction or zero degrees, and then the Moon as the faster one moves on. It starts to move through different angles like the aspects of 6 degrees, 30 degrees, 90 degrees (always as seen from the Earth) and so on until they meet again, once the Moon has covered the distance of the entire circle and moves up from behind to conjunct the Sun again.[44]

Each distance or each aspect has a certain quality, which gets interpreted by astrologers in a reading. Over the years, I had collected a lot of material and personal notes on the aspects because their geometry and numerology fascinated me. I suspected that the aspects could have something to do with the use of the magical numbers in wonder tales, such as three, seven, or nine.

So, for example, a 90 degree angle is the circle divided by four, producing a square in the circle. Divided by three it produces a triangle, consisting of three 120 degree aspects. While it is said that 90 degree aspects are full of tension, 120 degree aspects are interpreted as bringing good fortune and being very helpful. Divided by five produces five 72 degree angles and a five-pointed star shows. These aspects are interpreted as being full of creative energy, where man is shaping the world he lives in. The circle can be divided in as many parts as we wish, and astrologers try to gain insights from as many aspects as possible.

---

44 The lunation cycle is the most commonplace example of an unfolding of the aspect circle between two planets. Every New Moon marks the start of another 29 ½-day cycle between two encounters of the Sun and the Moon. As the Moon wanders on after a New Moon it reflects the Sun's light in ever different ways. The Sun and the Moon meet at their conjunction at New Moon (zero degrees), then the Moon, which moves thirteen times faster, travels on through the Crescent Moon Phase (45 degrees), on to the First Quarter Moon (90 degrees), on to the Gibbous Moon (135 degrees), on to the Full Moon (180 degrees). This is the point of opposition between the Sun and the Moon. Then, in the second half of the cycle, the Moon wanders on, entering the Disseminating Phase (225 degrees), the Third Quarter Phase (270 degrees), the Balsamic Phase (315 degrees), until it conjoins again with the Sun to enter the New Moon Phase (zero degrees) again. For further information see Dane Rudhyar's "The Lunation Cycle: A Key to the Understanding of Personality or Lunation Planning, Nature's Own Management Tool" by Michael R. Meyer, Kindle edition.

Is the Aspect Circle Telling a Story?

The more I looked at the astrological interpretation of aspects, the clearer it became that they were telling a story. The renowned late astrologer Dane Rudhyar even talked about a "journey," and he was looking at astrological aspects as telling a story. In Michael R. Meyer's "Rudhyar Archival Project"[45] I found further information on this fascinating idea. To give you an example, this is what Rudhyar wrote about some of the aspects:[46]

Two planets meeting at zero degrees: A new development process is starting. It contains a disorientation. There is an incapability to distinguish between inner wishes, dreams, feelings, and the outside reality.

The angles from zero degrees to 30 degrees (which are not defined closer): A new potential is set free. They show the existential necessity to consider new possibilities. The pressure of the past is met. One must try to overcome it, to at least psychologically disable the ghosts of the past.

Two planets 30 degrees apart: There comes a vague indication of where the journey will go. As undefined as it might still be, it holds a promise of a better future.

Two planets 45 degrees apart: The imaginative and active momentum is tested. Whenever somebody takes a step to a future fulfillment, or even just considers it, something is rebelling, as if there was a backward resistance. Insecurity or indecisiveness are expressions of old fears on the inside. There is also resistance that suddenly comes from the

---

45 khaldea.com/rudhyar/

46 Taken and translated from the book "Astrological Aspects: A Process-Oriented Approach," Dane and Leyla Rudhyar, Aurora Press, 1980

outside, the "real world," as the new inner vision must be adjusted to the outer reality.

The angles from 30 degrees to 60 degrees (which are not defined closer): In this phase, the initially freed potential must become central. It calls up resistance, which must be overcome.

Two planets 60 degrees apart: A synthesis happens, a developmental step is taken, talent is activated.

The angles from 60 degrees to 90 degrees (which are not defined closer): In this phase, actions as well as reactions need to be integrated into a broader field of activity.

In the attempt to further explore this fascinating cyclical story, I needed to consult other authors as well, extract the essence for each aspect, and compare it to my own observations. What helped me tremendously were Michael R. Meyer's detailed interpretation of 36 aspects of the entire developmental cycle,[47] Dusty Bunker's "Quintiles and Tredeciles, The Geometry of the Goddess," as well as John Addey's and David Hamblin's work on the harmonics, Robert P. Blaschke's, Ricki Reeves, and Emma Belle Donath's books.[48]

When listing the essence of each aspect, soon a story emerged. It spoke of initial difficulties, visions of a better future, and doors that

47 Check out Michael R. Meyer's eon on khaldea.com/eon/eonintro.shtml

48 "Harmonics in astrology: An introductory textbook to the new understanding of an old science" by John Addey, Cambridge Circle,1977; "Harmonic Charts: Understanding and Using the Principle of Harmonics in Astrological Interpretation" by David Hamblin, Harper Collins, 1987; "Astrology, A Language of Life, Volume II – Sabian Aspect Orbs" by Robert P. Blaschke, Earthwalk School of Astrology, 2000, and "Minor Aspects between Planets" by Emma Belle Donath, American Federation of Astrologers, 2012; "The Quindecile, The Astrology & Psychology of Obsession" by Ricki Reeves, Llewellyn Publications, 2001. I also found some minor aspects on the internet and did not take note of their source, unfortunately. Please let me know if you recognize a source so that I can quote it properly.

opened to new possibilities, plus moments of setbacks and phases of smooth sailings. At that point in my research, I became very excited again and eagerly tried to fill in the blanks. If only people's life stories could be told in this way!

Depending on the number the circle got divided by, the aspects had different qualities, as mentioned above. The *quintiles* (division of the circle by five) had to do with creative efforts, while the *septiles* (division of circle by seven) had to do with spiritual encounters, and the *octiles* (division of circle by eight) brought moments of suspense and tension. Thus, the essence of each aspect became a key sentence. I listed as many as I could from 0 degree to 360 degrees and started to compare them to the storyline of wonder tales.

Soon enough, I found signs of accord between the wonder tales and my aspect key sentences, and it quickly showed that I was on to something. However, it was very important to me that I did not alter any of the folklore texts. Preferably, the tales would have to be in their original version, as first collected from an oral storyteller. Also, I did not allow myself any turning around of sentences in the tales to make my "aspect-story" fit. On the contrary, I wanted to see whether *the exact order* of the storyline was matching *the exact order* of the aspect circle.

As I compared multiple wonder tales side-by-side, I found not only that the storylines matched, but that the tales also enriched my key sentences with images. This way, I could complete the regular astrological interpretations. Furthermore, I found additional aspects hidden in the tales. For example, around the 130-degree angle I noticed that the fairy tale protagonists always came to a *crossroad*s, where they needed to make an important decision. I came to call it *destiny's crossroads*.

Chapter 13

Another Access to Fairy Tales

"What you seek is seeking you."

Rumi

I started to comprehend the fairy tales in an entire new way. *The astrological key sentences indicated the path a story followed.* It was difficult, however, to clear-cut the aspect statements and keep them separate. A path as well as a story could be divided into segments, but where did one segment end and the next one start? The more aspects I found though, the clearer the image of each path segment became.

Let me show you what came out when I applied it to the already familiar tale "Mother Holle." It revealed another access to the tale. The tale does not go full circle, only from zero to 180 degrees, however. Like so many tales as I noticed, it ends in a common place at 180 degrees, where the key sentence says: "Manifestation and acknowledgement of the new status by the environment". It implies that all is said and done and the chances for a happy future are set up.

Mother Holle	Aspects
There was once a widow who had two daughters—one of whom was pretty and industrious, whilst the other was ugly and idle. But the mother was much fonder of the ugly and idle one, because she was her own daughter. And the other, who was a stepdaughter, was obliged to do all the work of the house.	**0 degree (Rudhyar):** A new development process is starting. It contains a disorientation. There is an incapability to distinguish between inner wishes, dreams and feelings and the outside reality. **(My key sentence):** Life is incomplete, a notion that triggers an in-limbo state, resulting in feelings of isolation and separation.
Every day the poor girl had to sit by a well, along the road, and spin and spin till her fingers bled.	**6 degrees** (**my key sentence):** A vision of a complete reality is harbored. *(By sitting by a well, which is the goddess's realm and "spinning till her fingers bled," the girl's closeness to the heavenly spinning/weaving cycles is implied. It shows that she is harboring the vision to spin a better future.)*
Now it happened that one day the shuttle was marked with her blood, so she dipped it in the well, to wash the mark off, but it dropped out of her hand and fell to the bottom. She began to weep and ran to her stepmother and told her of the mishap. But she scolded her sharply, and was so merciless as to say, "Since you have let the shuttle fall in, you must fetch it out again."	**12 degrees** (**my key sentence):** New opportunities come up. They offer to make this vision a reality.

So, the girl went back to the well, and did not know what to do. And in the sorrow of her heart, she jumped into the well to get the shuttle.	**18 degrees (Donath):** A door between two worlds. (**My key sentence):** Destiny's gate stands wide open and calls the human to go change what desperately needs to be changed. The hope for a quick fix is enticing.
She lost her senses. And when she awoke and came to herself again, she was in a lovely meadow where the sun was shining, and many thousands of flowers were growing.	**25.71 degrees (my key sentence):** A glance at the missing quality is given. What may have been dormant due to social conditionings is being re-awoken. *(The missing quality is a paradise-like state of being, where there is peaceful beauty and abundance.)*

Across this meadow she went, and at last she came to a baker's oven full of bread, and the bread cried out, "Oh, take me out, take me out, or I shall burn! I have been baked a long time."	**30 degrees (Rudhyar)**: Some of the potential that was triggered at the beginning of the cycle has "to go to work" now. There comes a vague indication of where the journey will go. As undefined as it might still be, it holds a promise of future fulfillment. (**My key sentence):** With the recognition of completeness also comes the sudden awareness of what has been missing all along. *(Since here the missing quality shows, we get a hint at what truly is missing from the girl's life: Meaningful action that does not let her finger bleed, but brings forth something of value like a manifested, life-sustaining loaf of bread. The act of baking was considered a sacred creational act, where masculine and feminine energies came together to bring forth something new. So, next to the real act of baking, there is also fertility and having children implied, since the oven is also a motherly symbol, a place, where the mysterious transformation from intangible to tangible happens.)*

So, she went up to it, and took out all the loaves one after another with the bread-shovel.	**36 degrees (Meyers):** This early and subjective phase carries an easily disregarded opportunity to participate in creative tomorrows; to envision and embody a new quality of being in substance. (**My key sentence):** A surge of optimism and a feeling of omnipotence entice to move on. **40 degrees (Blaschke):**... an awareness of the care and effort required to nurture any form of beauty into full manifestation. (**My key sentence):** Mostly unnoticed, the potential for completeness is growing.

After that, she went on till she came to a tree covered with apples, which called out to her, "Oh, shake me, shake me! We apples are all ripe." So, she shook the tree till the apples fell like rain, and went on shaking till they were all down, and when she had gathered them into a heap, she went on her way.	**45 degrees (Rudhyar)**: The imaginative and active momentum is tested. Whenever somebody takes a step to a future fulfillment, or even just considers it, something is rebelling, as if there was a backward resistance. Insecurity or indecisiveness are expressions of old fears on the inside. There is also resistance that suddenly comes from the outside, the "real world," as the new inner vision must be adjusted to the outer reality. **(My key sentence):** The hope for a new future triggers the impulse to move on, but at the same time, old patterns are pulling back. *(Apples stand for creation and procreation, as well. They are a symbol of love, marriage, and power. Two people come together and have the power to re-create. The apple tree, just like the oven, is a motherly symbol of transformation. The goddess sustains her children with food. By listening to the tree and doing what it says, the girl is showing her willingness to be part of the divine creation cycle.)*

At last she came to a little house, out of which an old woman peeped. But she had such large teeth that the girl was frightened and was about to run away.	**51.42 degrees (Meyer):** (...) affirming a creative future and illuminating the way to it with serendipity and seemingly chance encounters. **(My key sentence):** Support is given to advance matters. Depending on the degree of incompleteness, the missing quality can be perceived for what it truly is, or it is mistaken for something dangerous, evil or ugly. *(Here changes a mysterious encounter the course of the matter. "The missing quality can be seen for what it truly is" implies that the girl sees the mother of all, the goddess, which is at the same time her own power to re-create.)*
But the old woman called out to her, "What are you afraid of, dear child? Stay with me. If you will do all the work in the house properly, you shall be the better for it. Only you must take care to make my bed well and shake it thoroughly till the feathers fly—for then there is snow on the earth. I am Mother Holle."	**55 degrees (my key sentence):** Getting equipped to recover the missing quality. *(Now, she gets taught what it means to participate in the creative process by the goddess herself.)*
As the old woman spoke so kindly to her, the girl took courage and agreed to enter her service. She attended to everything to the satisfaction of her mistress	**60 degrees (Rudhyar):** A synthesis happens, a developmental step is taken, talent is activated. **(My key sentence):** Getting to know the surroundings. Something potentially life-changing is beginning to take shape.

and always shook her bed so vigorously that the feathers flew about like snowflakes. So, she had a pleasant life with her with never an angry word.	**72 degrees (Bunker):...** latent talents that can unfold during this lifetime. It is the light we carry within that can be activated or manifested during our life. **(My key sentence):** New and creative ways of interacting with the surroundings.
And to eat she had boiled or roast meat every day.	**80 degrees (Blaschke):** Those with this aspect may be drawn by spiritual conscience to participate in labor (...) for the welfare of the working class. **(My key sentence):** A protective sphere is provided to further strengthen the connection to the missing quality. *(As the girl contributes to the creative process and learns about the cycles, she is well-sustained and under protection of the goddess.)*
She stayed some time with Mother Holle, before she became sad. At first, she did not know what was wrong with her, but eventually found that it was homesickness. Although she was many thousand times better off here than at home, still she had a longing to be there.	**90 degrees (Meyer):** Maturing new qualities demand freedom from the past and its compulsions: **(My key sentence):** A threshold is crossed. The old must be left behind now. *(The girl knows that she cannot stay in Mother Holle's realm, for she will have to go home and apply what she learned. She will have to cross the threshold back into her real world.)*

At last she said to the old woman, "I have a longing for home, and however well off I am down here, I cannot stay any longer. I must go up again to my own people."	**102.85 degrees (Rudhyar/ Blaschke):** The power of the will in shaping character. It may bring intense life experiences that test the will and character. **(My key sentence):** Struggle and isolation are making the missing quality painfully evident. Yet it is here where the reconnection to the missing can be permanently established. *(As nice as it is at Mother Holle's she knows that what she learned needs to be brought back to her world.)*
Mother Holle said, "I am pleased that you long for your home again, and as you have served me so well, I myself will take you up again." Thereupon she took her by the hand and led her to a large door.	**105 degrees (my key sentence):** The ground is being prepared for something unusual to happen.

The door was opened, and just as the maiden was standing beneath the doorway, a heavy shower of golden rain fell, and all the gold clung to her, so that she was completely covered with it.	**108 degrees (Bunker):** The light you carry that can be expressed in this lifetime will surely lie beyond your physical body as a measure of who you were and what you did. It is your contribution to the creative pool of the universe. **(My key sentence):** A life-sustaining elixir is found or given. It is setting free a before-unknown inner strength, which stems from the growing connection to the formerly missing quality. *(The elixir is a golden aura, which is a sign of her being aware of the divine workings. Her connection to the divine will bring her good luck.)*
"You shall have that because you have been so industrious," said Mother Holle, and at the same time she gave her back the shuttle which she had let fall into the well. Thereupon the door closed, and the maiden found herself up above upon the earth, not far from her mother's house.	**115 degrees (my key sentence):** New hope is gained, and again careful discernment is required. *(She receives her shuttle back, which symbolizes that she now is aware of the cosmic cycles and will be able to weave her own destiny with careful discernment.)*
And as she went into the yard the cock was sitting on the well, and cried, "Cock-a-doodle-doo! Your golden girl's come back to you!"	**120 degrees (Blaschke):** Ease of expression, easy flow of energy… heart-mind integrative process. **(My key sentence):** The promise of fulfillment can be felt, which now drives forward.

So, she went in to her mother, and as she arrived thus covered with gold, she was well-received, both by her mother and her sister.	**130 degrees (my key sentence):** Arriving at destiny's crossroads. It is a turning point, the result of former efforts. Is the formerly missing quality now acknowledged? This crossroads is holding the promise to purposefully reshape fate, if the newfound quality can be upheld and carried on from now on.
The girl explained all that had happened to her, and as soon as the mother heard how she had come by so much wealth, she was very anxious to obtain the same good luck for the ugly and lazy daughter. That daughter had to seat herself by the well and spin. And in order that her shuttle might be stained with blood, she stuck her hand into a thorn bush and pricked her finger. Then she threw her shuttle into the well and jumped in after it.	**135 degrees (Rudhyar):** To succeed it is important to always be in harmony with the essence of the inner vision and include the needs of the others. It might require courage and persistence since there might be many personal fights. **(My key sentence):** The opportunity to purposefully reshape fate comes with the requirement to think and act differently. The intensifying energies have to be courageously faced, since the process will also provoke the surfacing of shadows. *(Her sister gets the same chance to spin her destiny in the realm of the goddess, but her prerequisites are bad to start out with.)*

Golden Mary's story ends here, and the focus moves to her sister. Normally, Golden Mary's story would go on and show her experiences when implementing her gained knowledge. In this case, astrology reveals that the two step-sisters symbolize the same person. The key sentences of the aspect circle continue in the same neutral or positive tone, meanwhile the tale shows what could go wrong, if bad habits prevail instead. The aspect circle is therefore used to emphasize a second time what it would take to recover the missing paradise-like state, while at the same time demonstrating the consequences when there is no awareness and little willingness to evolve.

She came, like the other, to the beautiful meadow and walked along the very same path. When she got to the oven, the bread again cried, "Oh, take me out, take me out, or I shall burn! I have been baking a long time." But the lazy thing answered, "As if I had any wish to make myself dirty!" And on she went. Soon she came to the apple tree, which cried, "Oh, shake me, shake me! We apples are all ripe."	**144 degrees (Bunker):** Those who will be saved through rebirth. **(My key sentence):** A relapse to the past can and must be avoided now if the right effort is made. Calm inward focus helps to be clearly determined and not to fall back into old habits. *(This is the moment of rebirth, however, to be transformed one must behave differently and avoid acting like in the past. Awareness for the right action at the right time is needed.)*
But she answered, "You wish! One of you might fall on my head," and so went on.	**150 degrees (Meyer):** (...) now comes a last chance for realignment, or at least an opportunity to make the best of the situation and to execute some kind of damage control. If a mostly futureward attitude has directed the course of unfoldment, this phase offers opportunities for improvement and the eradication of flaws. **(My key sentence):** Tensions are high and growth is happening quickly. No matter what is being done, whether actions and reactions happen out of trust or fear, they amplify the inner attitude.

When she came to Mother Holle's house, she was not afraid, for she had already heard of her big teeth, and she hired herself to her immediately.	**154.28 degrees (Blaschke):** The penetration of the veil of material reality into the astral realm and opening channels of communication between the individual and his spirit guides. **(My key sentence):** Direct exposure to the mysterious, transcending forces at work. It serves to experience their vast power and become familiar with their laws.
The first day she forced herself to work diligently, and obeyed Mother Holle when she told her to do anything, for she was thinking of all the gold that Mother Holle would give her. But on the second day, she began to be lazy, and on the third day still more so, and then she would not get up in the morning at all. Neither did she make Mother Holle's bed as she ought and did not shake it so as to make the feathers fly. Mother Holle was soon tired of this and gave her notice to leave.	**160 degrees (Blaschke):...** bringing into concrete manifestation the sincere prayer of the heart.... **(My key sentence):** Witnessing the divine workings. The potential of a wholesome life is unfolding. The opportunity presents itself to contribute to a more balanced human reality. *(Now would be her moment to change destiny and contribute to the divine creation process. What lies dormant in her as a talent should be brought to manifestation now.)*
The lazy girl was willing enough to go and thought that now the golden rain would come. Mother Holle led her also to the great door, but while she was standing beneath it, instead of the gold, a big kettleful of pitch was emptied over her.	**165 degrees (Reeves):** Through a process of awareness combined with a conscious effort to adjust and modify the energies involved, we are provided with an opportunity to utilize this dynamic to our benefit. **(My key sentence):** Fulfillment draws near. *(There is no judgment in how fulfillment looks like. It is the natural consequence of former efforts.)*

So, the lazy girl went home, but she was quite covered with pitch, and the cock on the well, as soon as he saw her, cried out - "Cock-a-doodle-doo! Your dirty girl's come back to you." But the pitch clung fast to her and could not be got off as long as she lived.	**180 degrees (Rudhyar):** The total concentration required for reaching any spiritual goal. **(My key sentence):** Manifestation and acknowledgement of the new status by the environment. Power is gained or lost again as a consequence of not being willing to contribute to a life that accounts for all qualities in the divine creative process.

(Please see "Beauty and the Beast" in Appendix B to get a demonstration of the full aspect circle from zero to 360 degrees.)

Looking at a fairy tale's deeper meaning, by considering its aspect build-up, revealed a whole new dimension hidden in the tale. It was not that Pitch Mary was a bad person and deserved bad luck, rather she was not at all aware of anything missing, nor was she willing to evolve much. If she had, she would have been attuned to what needed to be done at the right time. For Neolithic people on the verge of becoming farmers, it must have been very important to have a strong feel for the right timing. Action had to be taken in a certain order to have a successful outcome. The act of baking contained many steps from growing wheat to grinding it, to adding water, salt, and yeast, to kneading the dough, and letting it rise. When it finally was in the oven, it had to be taken out before it burned, otherwise all the effort would go to waste. The same was true with fruit on trees, as apples had to be plucked when ripe, for they couldn't be left hanging, otherwise they would eventually fall off and rot.

Therefore, it wasn't enough for Pitch Mary to go down the same road as Golden Mary. If she was unaware and did not make the right effort at the right time, she would be of no use to a lifestyle that depended on farming. But as we have seen, daily chores were never just ordinary chores, they always also had a spiritual dimension to them. Baking bread was also a sacred act of creating a physical "body," not unlike that of making a baby. Picking apples from the goddess's tree was a sign of willingness to contribute to manifesting life on the physical plane and to participate in the divine creative process.

The storyline of "Mother Holle," examined from an astrological point of view, therefore reveals that the tale speaks of a missing quality, a paradise-like state of being, with peaceful beauty and abundance, where humans participate in creating life in accordance with the divine. Golden Mary is open for this way of life and eager to learn how it can be achieved. Her knowledge and gained wisdom she brings back as her "riches."

The cock is the first to recognize her radiating golden aura of beauty and peace. Cocks are messengers between the worlds, just like the hag, because they are living in a "betwixt-and-between" place, between night and day. These places are said to be magical, because here the two realms meet. They can be physical places marking off one place from the other, like a hedge or a fence, or a sunny spot from the shade, or they define a special time, like between life and death (see "Hansel and Gretel"), or day and night. In this zone of twilight, human awareness is raised, and interaction between the worlds happens.

Even her stepmother acknowledges Golden Mary's emanating wisdom, learned from Mother Holle. The storyline shows that Pitch Mary would have had her fair chance to become a Golden Mary as well. However, her bad habits were preventing it from happening. Consequently, at the 180-degree aspect, where former actions have become a manifested reality, she, too, is acknowledged for her choices.

The tale demonstrates what it takes to co-create alongside Mother Nature, evolve, and become a wise leader. Pitch Mary could have learned it all as well, but her disinterest and old habits let her fall back into her old patterns at the 144-degree and the 160-degree aspects. "Karma is nothing but old habits", says astrologer Steven Forrest, and this rings true in this tale.

Chapter 14

The Moment of Revelation

"When the answer begins to come, it does so in a startling way . . . You will either see it or hear it and you are often given a great deal of knowledge in a brief period of time. It is a powerful experience that almost overwhelms you."

Frank Fools Crow

Aligning the fairy tales to the astrological aspect circle finally exposed the connection of the hero's journey to the cosmos. So, the tales displayed a cosmic order, which was hidden in their build-up. When I let that insight sit for a moment, I became aware of its vast consequences. It meant that even though the tales had been belittled as old wives' tales, altered in content to fit patriarchal values, or outright forbidden during the course of history, as soon as they were told in their universally valid cosmic rhythm, their astronomical message was smuggled into a society as if it were in a Trojan Horse. The wonder tales thus managed to survive despite new man-made laws; the cosmic laws did not go forgotten. Despite millennia of patriarchy with suppression of all feminine and natural, this astronomical truth got carried through the ages. What a stroke of genius on the part of our ancestors to construct tales that had such a capacity!

Patriarchy pushed the imbalance so far, and it had lasted for so long already, that equality between all beings, races, men, and women almost went forgotten. The Neolithic elders, shamans, astronomers, and bards thus managed to remind people of all epochs of *how a balanced and complete life* in alignment with the cosmic cycles could look and feel. The wonder tales provided people of all future epochs and ages with instructions on how to bring life back into alignment with nature, where there is love, renewal, and abundance for all. The tales demonstrate how divine creation works and that balance is a natural thing. But humanity has free will whether to attune to its creating and evolving rhythms. If people would rather ignore them, they settle for imbalance, which eventually expresses in hardships, as solidly proven in the millennia of patriarchy.

So, now the old wisdom of our Neolithic ancestors only needed to find application. However, even though I had found the alignment of the hero's journey to a cosmic cyclical pattern, I had no clue which wandering planets were responsible for triggering the aspect circle. Which two luminaries were writing somebody's personal heroic journey? I needed two reference points to tie the aspect circle to a personal chart. One point needed to serve as a starting point at zero degrees, and one as a marker to measure the ongoing wandering through the 360-degree circle.

For a long time already, I had been toying with the lunar nodes in people charts, because whenever something important happened in my life and in that of my clients, these two calculated points were prominent. The *lunar nodes* consisted of a *north node*, also called "the dragon's head" and a *south node* known as "the dragon's tail." Their observance allowed to accurately predict *eclipses*, which again were always involved in major life changes. I liked that the image of a dragon in the chart connected astrology with wonder tales.

Eclipses of the Sun and the Moon happen regularly. Our ancestors believed that there was an invisible dragon circling the sky, which only became visible during an eclipse when it cast its shadow over either the Moon or the Sun. The dragon was believed to thus appear as a shadow and eat the Sun or the Moon bite by bite, until there was only cold, and darkness left. People greatly feared the eclipses throughout the ages. The moment of decreasing light or increasing darkness and cold must have felt like Judgment Day to our forefathers. Eclipses were dreaded, and it sure helped to be prepared for those draconic encounters with destiny, when the fairy appeared on her dragon chariot like in "The Glass Fountain" tale.

Long the path, fast it's told, the storyteller would say, but eventually, it all started to fall into place. This was it. Finally, the solution to what I had been looking for all those years began to show. It had been under my nose for much of the time, but I could not recognize it. I first had to collect data over a long period of time and learn to view the world through the lens of prehistoric fairy tales, before I could see the pattern, which emerges only over a time span of roughly eighteen-and-a-half years.

The lunar nodes are travelling clockwise around a chart, and their movement resembles a rather regular weaving motion. It takes them 18.61 years for one full cycle. The "nodal axis," as it is also called, is used in astrological interpretation to determine the soul's development from past to future, from *south node* to *north node.* The lunar nodes were old acquaintances of mine, and I had been working with them in personal charts for many years. I had found much confirmation that there indeed was a connection between the south node and the soul's experience brought into this life from past lives. Since I had also worked as a regression therapist, I had been able to witness the soul's desire to take the gained experience and strive for the still hidden potential of the north node in many sessions.[49] Were the lunar nodes maybe describing a person's heroic journey, while the soul was spiraling upward toward more wisdom, away from past mistakes to a better future?

I took out all my old notes of client sessions and compared them. At the same time, I went through my own diaries and interviewed numerous people on what the American psychologist James Hillman would have called their soul biography. Quickly it showed that with the help of the same key sentences I used to examine wonder tales, I could question people about their real-life-stories. When tracking the journey of the lunar nodes, the developmental journey of our souls could be made out. The pieces of the puzzle fit. It was the position of the north node in a personal chart that provided the zero-degree position, where the hero's journey began at the time of birth. The transiting north node provided the information of the person's whereabouts along the road.

I couldn't believe it! After all these years of searching, I could finally tie the hero's journey of wonder tales to a birth chart. It was the path of the lunar north node which described a person's *life story*. Yet, it wasn't so much the obvious events such as a wedding or a relocation that made out the personal story. Rather it was the subtle, underlying, and hard to grasp sensations, emotions, and motivations, which got revealed

49 My personal experiences corresponded very much with Steven Forrest's book "Yesterday's Sky, Astrology and Reincarnation," Seven Paws Press, 2008. I highly recommend this book if you are interested in the matter.

when contemplating life with the help of aspect key sentences. It was the history of the soul that emerged, or as Hillman wrote *"the experiences arising from major dreams, crises, and insights (which) give definition to the personality."*

It seemed that people's soul history was subtly woven on the inside while they were busy doing other things. From time-to-time then, the inner network would become visible in an outside decision or manifestation. Using the key sentences, it was very much like finding deeper layers of meaning in a biography, just like when examining a fairy tale. Suddenly, biographies could be understood from the soul's perspective, which was encompassing in its nature. Hillman writes that these experiences "*too have 'names' and 'dates' like the outer events (...); they are like boundary-stones which mark out one's own individual ground.*"[50] I found that the lunar nodes were precisely marking such boundary-stones in life, which indicated a more hidden journey of the soul, not always congruent with outer events. Interestingly, Hillman's term "boundary-stone" proved very accurate in an almost uncanny way, as it showed later.

Always on a Heroic Journey

When it became clear that the indicator for the hero's journey were the lunar nodes, the riddle was finally solved. Their journey around a full aspect circle from zero to 360 degrees was what indicated our soul's developmental journey. This was our very own heroic story! My initial questions could be answered now: "*How do I know if I am on a hero's*

---

50 "Healing Fiction," James Hillman, Spring Publications, Woodstock, Connecticut, 1983

journey? If I am, where am I at? How and when does change occur? And what is the gain?"

Now, the lunar nodes take 18.61 years to complete one turn, which comes to 18 years 7 months and 9 days or a little over eighteen-and-a-half years. Therefore, a person can live through as many as five or six full developmental cycles, or *hero's journeys* in one lifetime, depending on the lifespan. Therefore, in the life of a person, every eighteen-and-a-half years a *new* heroic journey starts, which feeds off the experiences and choices made during the former cycles. One cycle builds onto the wisdom gained of the previous cycle and ideally increases a person's wisdom with increasing age.

Put into a table format, it looks like this:

The Hero's Journeys in a Person's Life	
1st Developmental Cycle	From birth to about 18½ years old
2nd Developmental Cycle	From about 18½ to about 37 years old
3rd Developmental Cycle	From about 37 to nearly 56 years old
4th Developmental Cycle	From nearly 56 to about 74½ years old
5th Developmental Cycle	From about 74½ to about 93 years old
6th Developmental Cycle	From about 93 to about 111½ years old

Now, it was obvious that *everybody* was always on a heroic journey, since the hero's journey was marking the biography of the soul as she developed over a lifetime. It was the path of evolution through life from birth to death, from a karmic past to a not yet manifested future.

Chapter 15

A Stone Circle with 56 Pillars

"For those who hold the Sun and the Moon in the right order, knowing the past and the future becomes simple and obvious."
Quote from Swara Yoga

In many European languages, the term "to tell a story" indicates that it has something to do with *counting* or *accounting*. The French, Italian, and Spanish words for storytelling can be traced back to the Latin word "computo," to compute. When French people tell a story, they "raconte une conte," which means they "re-count an enumeration." Italians call it: "raccontare un racconto," which means the same thing. The German verb "erzählen" contains the word "counting" and in English, the term "tall tales" implies a measurement as well.[51] So, when a tale is told, there is some form of *enumeration, calculation,* or *computation* going on. Isn't this exactly what happens when a wonder tale is told from aspect to aspect, from zero degree to 360 degrees? It *accounts* for each aspect, one after the other, as it is stringing together the entire story.

51 "Initiations et Contes de Fées" (The Initiatory Path in Fairy Tales, The Alchemical Secrets of Mother Goose), Bernard Roger, Dervy, 2013

It all fit. *It is the lunar nodes' cycle that gets enumerated when a wonder tale is told.* By telling it, one full cycle is being accounted for. As the lunar nodes progress through the aspect circle their journey was embellished with story-images that made the process easily understandable and relatable.

So, by now I knew that the lunar nodes' cycle made up the inner structure of wonder tales and that the tales were being told as a way of remembering this cyclical process. At the same time, logically the lunar nodes' cycle and its story, the hero's journey, was also applicable in real life.

But as much as everything fit, I could not explain how on earth the Neolithic "stone age" people, could possibly have known about such a thing as the lunar nodes. If the fairy tales were 6,000 years old, then the counting in the form of telling a story must be just as old. Unlike the Sun and Moon, the lunar nodes could not be observed in the sky. The north node and the south node are two invisible points; they are merely calculated. Yet, obviously the Neolithic people must have known about them, if wonder tales were accounting for their cyclical journeys. If I wanted to include this second, cosmic message of the fairy tales into my book, I would have to find an explanation how our Neolithic ancestors could have possibly tracked something in the sky that was not visible but only computable.[52]

52 The lunar nodes are the points of intersection where the Moon's orbital path intersects with the Sun's orbital path on the ecliptic. The place where the Moon crosses into the northern hemisphere is the north node and on the one opposite side, where it dips into the southern hemisphere is the south node.

Archeo-Astronomy

In my explorations, I received assistance from a relatively new field of study, the field of archeo-astronomy. Soon, I was to learn that the Neolithic people were highly skilled astronomers. According to archeo-astronomy, monuments such as Newgrange in Ireland or Stonehenge and Avebury in England were built by them and served as gigantic astronomical "computers." By considering astronomy at these sites, scientists are now starting to shed light on this previously unaccounted for feature of Megalithic buildings. Slowly but surely, their purpose is being revealed, and with it, insights into the Neolithic worldview are obtained.

Archeo-astronomy asks of a scientist to be willing to go out there during all seasons, always of the day and night, always with theodolite and measuring rope in hand, to make on-the-spot-observations and calculations of the celestial movements. One such archeo-astronomer is Robin Heath, whose body of work, accumulated over some thirty years, provided me with the answers I was looking for.[53]

Heath explained that the Neolithic people were "drawing down the heaven," meaning that the builders of Megalithic complexes were visually depicting what happened in the sky down on the face of the Earth. They were thus building a model on the ground of what they observed in the sky. The geometrical shapes, created by the celestial cycles, were scaled down and reproduced down on the ground. By "drawing" the cosmic cycles down, depicting it on the surface of the Earth, they created devices with several layers of function. They could compute calendars and at the same time use them as temples for people to gather, celebrate

53 "Sun, Moon and Stonehenge, Proto Stonehenge in Wales, Temple in the Hills and Bluestone Magic," Robin Heath, Bluestone Press, Wales, 1998-2016

and experience their being embedded in all of nature. The Neolithic people seemed to have wanted to better understand the life-shaping forces and act in alignment with them.

Megalithic sites therefore must have once been places of great wisdom. What happened in the sky was not seen as separate from what happened on the Earth, rather it must have been viewed as giving the necessary fertile impulses for the Earth to prosper.

Well, it turned out that there was indeed a former monument that used to compute the lunar nodes. It was an inconspicuous circle of fifty-six holes, which lay around the famous Megalithic site of Stonehenge. The Aubrey Circle, as this former stone circle is called, seemed to hold the answer to my question.

The Aubrey Circle

The Aubrey Circle was the first feature that was built at the site of Stonehenge about 5,000 years ago. It was erected 500 years prior to the Megalithic monument we know today and was named after John Aubrey, who in the 17th century detected its remnants. At that point, all that was left of it were fifty-six holes in the ground arranged in a circle. Archeological research found that what today are only holes once must have hosted fifty-six bluestone pillars.

Upon hearing that the Aubrey Circle was the large-scale Neolithic "computer" which calculated the movement of the lunar nodes, I decided I needed to visit this place. It held the answer as to how the originators of the wonder tales and hero's journey could have known of the lunar nodes.

Soon, I got the opportunity to take a short trip to England to see for myself. After a scenic drive on an extraordinary bright but cold day in mid-January, I got off the shuttle bus that brought visitors from the museum to the actual site of Stonehenge. After a short walk, the gigantic Megalithic rocks came into sight. An archeologist recently called it the "skyline of a prehistoric Manhattan," because, as excavations showed, it once attracted people from all over Europe. For our ancestors, this place used to be *the* place to go for trading and spiritual inspiration. What an amazing site!

My reason for coming here, though, was not the monument of gigantic size in front of me, but rather I was interested in the circle around it, the Aubrey Circle. I looked around and could recognize the large circular ditch the Neolithic astronomers had created as a first action around the site in about 3,000 BCE. The bank that resulted from digging the ditch was heaped up to form a circular wall allowing better observation of the horizon in this otherwise flat landscape. The area within the circle became a sacred space, as is every inner room of a circle. In my shamanic trainings, we usually formed a circle at the beginning of our healing work and stated our intention that "in this circle all is held, in this circle all is healed." It always had quite a comforting effect and when things got tough and emotional, the circle proved to be a place of security and resolution.

The Aubrey Circle used to compute and track the lunar nodes and their progress through the aspects, round and round the fifty-six bluestones. If all my research and the resulting conclusions proved correct, it is within this circle that the wonder tales were created and told, and then spilled into all of Europe. *Here, astronomy got embellished with the colorful dress of stories.*

The old Jewish parable "The Truth and the Folk Tale" came to mind, where truth to be understood *embellished herself with the clothes of folk tales* (see Chapter 2).

Since the lunar nodes are what links the dance of the Sun and the Moon to the Earth, they symbolize the *light and life* that manifests down on our material plane. Their creational energies bring forth all life on planet Earth. The Sun and the Moon keep producing the changing of day and night, dry and moist, summer and winter. So, here in this ancient sacred place, tales were told that talked in an embellished way about how the Sun and the Moon influenced all life on Earth.

It was rather crucial information for all beings inhabiting the planet. *The lunar nodes made the developmental rhythm of the solar and lunar energies visible.* Calculating them served to track their couple dance and brought awareness to their form-giving cycles. Who knew about their rhythm could stay attuned with the cyclical creation and therefore could collaborate with the divine. So, by tracking the lunar nodes, the Neolithic elders gained insights into how the cycles shaped personal lives and destinies.

Continuing this line of thought, they must have viewed *humans as manifested carriers of the solar and lunar energies* on the material earthly plane. Out of this, the idea of the human being as a "hero" must have been born. By tracking the cyclical dance and observing its effect on people's lives, the Neolithic elders were able to help people attune their lives to the cosmic cycles. Thus, a human, *a hero*, could increase his consciousness as he walked through life under the ever-shaping influence of the divine creational energies.

It became clear to me, more than ever, that Neolithic people were no "stone age people who drug their wives around by the hair." To the contrary, these builders of Megalithic monuments were highly sophisticated astronomers and shamans. They not only established places, "temples," where people could expose themselves to the divine creative energies, they also clothed their observations into stories of deep wisdom to raise people's awareness.

Thus, folk once gathered here at the site, not to hear some abstract astronomical lectures, no, they came to have a profound spiritual experience. When a wonder tale was told, the cosmic order could be felt. It was illustrated by stories of heroes who walked in alignment with the cycles. The stories went straight from the ears to the heart, where they activated the emotional centers of the listeners. New connections were built between their nerve cells, which again promoted feelings of compassion, hope and inspiration for a happy and balanced future.

A Balanced Soli-Lunar Calendar

So, here I was standing now, inside the circular bank of Stonehenge, trying to imagine the middle space empty, only surrounded by fifty-six bluestone pillars. Nowadays, instead of stone pillars there were only fifty-six holes, which were filled in, and of those, only three were marked.

I was quite disappointed to find the Aubrey Circle so undervalued at this site. In fact, the Aubrey Circle was so strikingly inconspicuous next to the gigantic rocks that it reminded me of the underrated

European folk tales, both holding the wisdom of our indigenous ancestors, both unrecognized for what they were. Here, all eyes were on the large rocks, just as all eyes were on the written myths.

So, while everybody else was taking pictures of the giant rock formation, I aimed my camera at the ground to at least take some pictures of these three markers. The tourists around me looked questioningly at me, especially when they saw me jumping up and down to get an idea of the circle's size. It was huge. Only the black ravens sitting high up on the rocks in the middle seemed to understand my strange behavior. They tilted their heads curiously toward me, watching my every move.

I imagined the bluestone pillars still in place in the Aubrey Circle and tried to visualize the Neolithic method of cycle tracking. An astronomer or shaman, whatever they were called back then, moved—with or without much ceremony—a marker from one stone to the next. Maybe it was a colored piece of cloth, a set of feathers, a wreath or something else which they placed on or around a pillar. One such marker was used for the Moon and was moved counterclockwise every day at sunrise and then again at sunset. Another marker was used for the Sun and moved every thirteen days.[54] By means of this method, the position of the Sun and the Moon could be read in any kind of weather, as well as the phase of the Moon and the season. Then came the markers for the lunar nodes. They were put on two pillars opposite each other and shifted clockwise every four months. Thus, "the dragon" could be tracked and eclipses predicted. It was one large timekeeping calendar. So simple and so elegant.[55]

54 By using 56 pillars, not only 28, an accuracy of 99.8 % could be obtained. (Robin Heath cura.free.fr/decem/06heath.html)

55 "Sun, Moon and Stonehenge," Robin Heath, Bluestone Press, 1999, or consult his presentation "The Marriage of the Sun and Moon" at cura.free.fr/decem/06heath.html for details.

Imagining that the Aubrey Circle once had such a function was difficult to grasp, and I sat down on a bench in front of the impressive Megalithic monument of Stonehenge. I took out my worn copy of Heath's book "Sun, Moon and Stonehenge." Heath wrote that the calendar produced here at the Aubrey Circle reflected the *actual cosmic cycles as they were happening in the sky*. Tracking their annual journeys, it became evident that there are *thirteen* months in one year and that the Moon moves *thirteen* times faster than the Sun. This meant that, of course, the thirteenth month of the Moon had to be considered since it is a natural fact. 13 months of 28 days make a year of 364 days, which divides into 4 seasons of 91 days and a 7-day week. A year with 364 days, however, eventually moves out of astronomical alignment with the seasonal cycles, because the Earth's orbit is not perfectly circular. Therefore, from time-to-time adjustment is needed by adding extra days.[56] The Aubrey Circle at Stonehenge is precisely such a well-balanced soli-lunar calendar, a calendar of 364 days. Here, the Moon and the Sun cycles were depicted *exactly as they were*, in their naturally balanced alternation.

The calendar therefore also must have served to track a human's journey through life. Human beings, who eventually came to be called *hero*, because they were the Great Mother's divine child and walked the Earth as her representative, must have aimed at keeping up their good fortune. By staying aligned with the soli-lunar cycles they could always remain healthy and in touch with the divine. The term "hero" in German, "Held," is etymologically connected to the Old Norse word "heill"

56 Intercalary days are days that are inserted in the calendar to harmonize it with factual astronomy, see also "Sun, Moon and Stonehenge," Robin Heath, Bluestone Press, 1998

for "luck," "good omen" or "good fortune," and the English word "health" is connected to it as well. So, a calendar that helped the human stay on track with his good luck was a mighty good thing indeed.[57]

57 Still 2,700 years after the construction of the Aubrey Circle, a hero was a human of divine origin, who could do service to mankind. See Hesiod, about 700 BCE and en.wiktionary.org/wiki/held
Only later did the meaning of "hero" change to stand for "somebody who fights and protects."

Chapter 16

The Problem with the Number Thirteen

"It is clear that myth may provide evidence of ancient astronomical knowledge, while astronomy may also provide an additional perspective on ancient myths."

Robin Heath

So, originally *a hero* was a human who was exposed to the shaping influences of the Sun and the Moon while incarnated on planet Earth. By "computing" the lunar nodes with the help of stone circles such as the Aubrey Circle at Stonehenge, the journey of the hero could be mapped out and clothed in stories. Magical stories they were, wonder tales, demonstrating how a life under the balanced calendar could be. A calendar where the Sun and Moon were "married" in equal terms had the wondrous capacity to guide a hero through a life full of marvels, good luck, and health.

Calendars are still based on the Sun and the Moon, only we modern people have become unaware of it. However, here comes the million-dollar question: Why are we then using a calendar today that does *not* account for the cycles as they *are happening in the sky?* What I first thought to be a hairsplitting detail turned out to be at the very root of the patriarchal problem, according to archeo-astronomer Robin Heath. Even though we might think it does not really matter whether we calculate time by this or that method, *it matters a lot,* so I learned. In fact, it makes an enormous difference. Using today's 365-day calendar does *not* allow for the integration of both solar *and* lunar cycles! It entirely dismisses the lunar cycle and disconnects the month from its actual cosmic length. With twelve solar months per year, the length of a month is dictated by the Sun. In this kind of calendar, the months are viewed as going from one *New Moon* to the next *New Moon*. The Moon therefore only gets acknowledged by her meetings with the mighty Sun and loses her own individuality. However, the Moon can be observed to return at least thirteen times per year to the same position in the sky.

This small shift of perception results in large-scale consequences. Our awareness gets separated that the Sun and the Moon belong together, since they are *both* involved in creating nature on Earth. An observer on the face of the Earth would get to witness a beautiful relationship up in the sky, an elegant *weaving* of the Sun and the Moon around her viewpoint. Tying their points of intersection, the lunar nodes, down to the Earth by means of observation would then link the observer to that which she observes, letting her become a third party in the weaving dance. In other words, she who is aware of the Sun-Moon cycles holds their threads in her hands and participates in life's weaving.

However, not considering the cycles as they are occurring in the sky means forfeiting that chance to co-weave destiny and promotes a passive watching of a solo artist up in the sky, the Sun, dancing all to himself. The "weaving" gets interrupted and allows for ideas such as the Sun alone being responsible for all life on Earth. One thread alone makes no weaving, though. Yet, such ideas laid the ground for bizarre concepts such as male gods who give birth, like *Zeus* giving birth to *Athena* from his skull or rescuing the fetal *Dionysus*, by sewing him into his thigh and giving birth to him a few months later.

It is no easy thing to synchronize solar to lunar cycles and to deal with the *"mismatch of about a third of a lunation between the end of twelve lunations (the lunar year) and the end of the solar year,"*[58] and it is much easier to just calculate with the number *twelve*. It divides in many parts and helps to smoothly sort time, unlike the lunar number *thirteen*, which cannot be divided, because it is a prime number. So, the number thirteen was discarded and the number twelve became "king."

The Greek Zeus was, like his later roman counterpart Jupiter, considered to be the heavenly god, the god of the daytime sky. His name indicated a bright shining quality, like that of the Sun, and he was said to govern the regulation of time, the changing of seasons. So, suddenly there was the Greek pantheon with twelve Olympian gods, the council of twelve Roman gods, Jupiter being their king, probably because the planet Jupiter takes twelve years to return to the same position in the sky. The solar wheel of the Celtic god Taranis had twelve spokes and Israel had twelve tribes and Jesus twelve apostles. All these later myths reflected the new emphasis on the number twelve, discarding the lunar number thirteen altogether. So, obviously over time the idea grew that the Sun alone was responsible for the cyclical changes on Earth.

58 Robin Heath on skyscript.co.uk/moonheath.html

Therefore, living by the 365-day calendar causes the disconnection from the lunar cycles and qualities altogether and gives room for *solar* solo dancers.

Thirteen is by its nature a very lunar number, since the Moon moves just over *13 degrees a day* and it travels this orbit *thirteen times* each year. There are *13 months* of 27 days 7 hours and 43 minutes (called "the sidereal month") during one seasonal turnover. So, one could really say that the number thirteen is the number of the Moon.

However, once people started to prefer the golden Sun and its easily calculable number twelve, the solar-lunar balance started to tip in human awareness. Eventually it brought the trouble of the ignored and undervalued feminine attributes, injustice, and violence against women. It gave rise to a demonized lunar-feminine. Such a one-sided perception inevitably *must* cause trouble, because it lets the know-how of the creational cycles sink into oblivion. It interrupts the connection of humans to the creational energies so that they lose touch with their own true nature. They forget what it is that sustains them on the physical plane.

Wonder tales inform us that it is only the sacred marriage between female and male energies, yin and yang, the Moon and the Sun, which brings forth growth and new life. With it comes balance and happiness. "*They got married, had children, and lived happily ever after,*" many a tale ends. If we do not take into account the natural fact of a balanced Sun-Moon calendar, we need not be surprised if there will be a severe imbalance in life, often expressed in tales mentioning a fertility problem or a problem to feed the children (as we have seen in "Hansel and Gretel"). The Grimm Brothers' tale "Sleeping Beauty" begins like this: "*A long time ago there were a king and queen who said every day, ah, if only we had a child, but they never had one."*

Heath mentioned this tale to be such an example. In "Sun, Moon and Stonehenge" he shows that this tale clearly demonstrates what a change in calendars can cause when the thirteenth month gets suppressed.

Sleeping Beauty

In "Sleeping Beauty," or "Briar Rose," as this famous story is also called, the king only had twelve golden plates and therefore only invited twelve fairies to his daughter's christening feast. (Christianity already favored the new calendar and the number twelve). The twelve golden plates are the symbols for twelve solar months per year, when the length of a month is dictated by the Sun.

The thirteenth fairy comes nevertheless (the lunar months are a cosmic fact, they cannot simply be ignored), makes her prophesy, and the king then tries to hide all spinning wheels in his kingdom. Everybody in the kingdom is therefore ordered to forget about the cosmic spinning and weaving of the Sun and Moon cycles. They now must live by the king's man-made law of only accepting the Sun and twelve months in a calendar.

Well, it takes no evil fairy making a spell to see that this had to end in disaster. There can be no earthly law over the cosmic order, not even a king's laws. Eventually, the princess finds out. She finds a spinning wheel, pricks her finger, and falls into a deep sleep. The spinning wheel she finds symbolizes an observatory circle with spokes that divide the sky into sections like that of the Aubrey Circle with its stone pillars. It is a symbol that must have been easily understood by the Neolithic listener. The princess inevitably got into contact with the cosmic cycles as they naturally occur, since the lunar rhythm inside of her body was becoming very noticeable in puberty with the menstruation cycle setting in.

But the solo rulership of male patriarchy is strong. The king's laws and the entire organization of his court are set to blend out all that has to do with *thirteen*, the lunar quality. Inevitably, it drifts into the oblivion, into the shadow, and goes forgotten over time. So now, as the princess meets the spinning wheel and the natural cosmic order, she cannot just cry out: "Look what I found!" It is a taboo that is broken, which most likely will get the death penalty in such a king's realm. So rather than acknowledge the fact that the lunar principle has been suppressed and ignored for years, the entire kingdom goes to sleep. Over time, there will be no more words for the lunar quality. It will become mysterious and demonic as it secretly moves the fluids of the Earth. The image of the evil dragon sitting inside of mountains and seas is not far. So, rather than to acknowledge the presence of the thirteenth fairy, the lunar and feminine cycle, the society bends to the king's new rule of twelve and wanders into the deep sleep of oblivion. The princess could not become a rebel on her own and shake things up in her father's kingdom, because she is not familiar yet with the lunar quality. She grew up with this taboo, in a society which guarded the lunar as a secret until it was nearly forgotten. When she first felt its presence, it was a sting, a shock, an overwhelming moment of alignment with the cosmos. Maybe it also felt like the coming home into the embrace of the mother, the slumber must have been sweet and comforting.

Eventually, the princess got found because the cosmic wheels do turn, whether one decides to live by them or not. Every so often, the chance presents itself to be resurrected. Luckily, there are always people like the young prince who recognize the lunar quality when they see it. They are in alignment with the cosmic cycles and see the signs of beauty in nature such as the roses growing around the castle. A young prince capable of recognizing the lunar quality will be naturally living by a calendar which considers both lunar and solar cycles. He will not believe in dancing solo. He knows that true love, happiness, and abundance stem from an equal dance of the masculine with the feminine, and it is a sacred marriage. The princess will only want to wake up to a prince that acknowledges her lunar, feminine quality. It is her destiny, as predicted by the fairies. It is her destiny to bring back the awareness for the lunar cycles in her father's kingdom's calendar.

As I later found, this is *the basic issue* of the wonder tales, whether they spell it out directly or indirectly. It seemed to be the Neolithic elders' main concern to demonstrate the function of the balanced soli-lunar calendar and *to keep it active in people's minds by means of stories*, stories that showed the consequences of what happens if the lunar goes forgotten.

A New Era Under an Unbalanced Calendar

So, just like in "Sleeping Beauty", the balanced 364-day calendar fell into oblivion over time. The fifty-six bluestones were removed to serve another aim within the Stonehenge monument and the function of the Aubrey Circle was forgotten. Only the wonder tales remained intact in their true astronomical build-up, still reflecting the old balanced soli-lunar calendar. The Aubrey Circle became the Aubrey holes and were covered with grass until their re-discovery 4,000 years later by John Aubrey.

During this gradual shift, the Sun began to receive credit for its creative powers and all things lunar became more and more discredited. Soon, only the number *twelve* was sacred and the number *thirteen* became an unlucky number. *Solar heroes* were now worshipped and *thirty-three* became their number. This is because after thirty-three years the Sun returns to the same position in the sky. Emphasizing the thirty-three-year repeat cycle of the Sun meant that the Sun alone came to be acknowledged. It produced new myths such as the Celtic "Tuatha de Danaan," "The Gilgamesh," "Hercules," and Christian epics. Christ, for example, began his ministry at age thirty and was crucified at age thirty-three. Heath sees Christ's resurrection at age thirty-three as another calendrical metaphor.[59]

However, as we have seen, only considering the Sun-cycle inevitably brought major consequences for women and for humanity in general. With the rise of this one-sided perception, the *male* solar hero became the representative of the Sun who had to fight and protect. He became the knight in shining armor who brought light into the abyss of the feminine shadow zone. Consequently, the lunar qualities fell into a taboo existence. Life became a two-folded, polar principle: black and white, good and bad. Two opposites fighting each other, one superior to the other, and bringing on hell for the other. No longer was life viewed as an "as well as" principle, rather it became an "either/or" principle.

59 "Sun, Moon and Stonehenge," Robin Heath, Bluestone Press, 1998, see also online at cura.free.fr/decem/06heath.html

The beast, which once was the goddess (see "Beauty and the Beast" in Appendix B) had to be killed, so the mythological slaughter of the dragon began. This again eventually led to the slaughter of wise women, innocent girls, and healers of the old wisdom, who came to be called witches. By then, patriarchy and the new calendar had taken over for good.

A cold shiver ran down my spine and it was not just from the brisk January wind. I turned the page quickly. Heath mentioned that the final word on the calendar change from 364 to 365 days per year might have been caused by two ignorant Roman emperors with big egos:

"Unfortunately, in the modern world, we have adopted a rather less useful calendar based on 365 days—a solar dominated calendar originally imposed on the growing Empire by the Romans. The imposition of this calendar—the most astronomically close to the actual seasonal year – was in order to prevent the keepers of the calendar through outposts of the Roman Empire from forgetting to account for the intercalary days. So chaotic had this vital timekeeping process become that in 45 AD Sosigenes designed the Roman calendar, with one important departure from the calendar we still use today. He originally alternated 30 and 31-day months, apart from February, which had an interesting 28 days. Later, Caesar Augustus (August) in order to not appear any less than Julius Caesar added an extra day to the month named after him, thus breaking the sequence and providing the necessity for remembering the rhyme we all learn at school to learn the individual months lengths. Thus, it is true that the random egoism of a megalomaniac

Roman nearly two thousand years ago still determines just one of the many irrational aspects of modern timekeeping in the Space Age!"[60]

And look where we are now, 2,000 years later: we live in a terribly imbalanced world, the masculine valued higher than the feminine and the divine abundance distributed so unevenly. Yet, it is consoling that according to Heath, until the Middle Ages the 364-day calendar was still known and in use in Europe. My own findings confirm this, as presented in this book. The balanced calendar's wisdom was obviously preserved in the wonder tales, as the word "Mär" "message" in *Märchen* implies. On a closer look, there is even more behind that little word. It implies that it is, *"a piece of news or a message of something, an event or a truth, which is well-known or deserves to be well-known, so that it merits to be spread."*[61]

So, isn't this exactly what the Neolithic elders, who created the tales, must have had in mind: to spread the (maybe already well-known) *truth* of the Aubrey calendar into all of Europe?

Therefore, it is highly possible that the wonder tales were a Neolithic invention that intended to spread the astronomical knowledge of the balanced soli-lunar calendar. This creation obviously managed to smuggle its message of truth right by the solo dancing kings of history, the dark Middle Ages and its human devils, past the cruel witch-hunts and past the mechanical views of the Age of Reason. Undamaged it arrived in our modern times. What a performance. And what power must lie in such ancient wisdom.

---

60 "Sun, Moon and Stonehenge" by Robin Heath, Bluestone Press 1998, p. 43

61 "Die Märchen der Brüder Grimm, eine Einführung" (The Tales of the Brothers Grimm, an Introduction), Heinz Rölleke, Reclam, 2004 (translated by the author)

Chapter 17

Dancing with the Muse

"Had I the heavens' embroidered cloths,
Enwrought with golden and silver light,
The blue and the dim and the dark cloths
Of night and light and the half-light,
I would spread the cloths under your feet:
But I, being poor, have only my dreams;
I have spread my dreams under your feet;
Tread softly because you tread on my dreams."
William Butler Yeats

By now, I was sitting in the warm café at the Visitor Center of Stonehenge, reflecting on the wonder tales and the Neolithic mind. Every tale begins with a consequence that people must live with, when their societies do not consider Sun and Moon, masculine and feminine, as equal. They always make this imbalance their central issue. There might be an imbalance between polarities such as a poor farmer versus a rich king or a protagonist who has a hunch that something is missing and decides to go looking for it. During the story it becomes clear that their mission is to retrieve the missing lunar quality. It comes in all sorts of shapes, such as love, health, sustenance, water, salt, and so on, that is missing. The variations are nearly endless. Some spell out the calendar problem explicitly, others just hint at an imbalance, due to something missing.

Having immersed myself into the Neolithic astronomers' minds, I could not help but think they saw it coming back then. They must have recognized the signs of their time that patriarchy was on the rise due to such one-sided views and inevitably would cause an imbalance in the human thinking. Objects of copper and gold had been found by archeologists at Stonehenge, so we can imagine that traders from faraway places came to this buzzing European center of commerce. They must have brought this new kind of thinking right to the doorstep of the Neolithic elders, producing new sets of values. The tale "Hans in Luck" demonstrated this shift in values very clearly. For Hans, a lump of gold was still nothing but a nice, shiny object, too heavy and unpractical to carry. However, in the eyes of his trading partner, it had a different value and he gladly gave his horse for it. At that moment, Hans had more use for a horse, to him it was a method of transportation, whereas the lump of gold he would have to schlep around for nothing. However, the Age of Metallurgy had begun and there were people out there who knew what to do with a lump of gold. The old matriarchal values, which were aligned with the natural cosmic balance, were in jeopardy. The lump of gold resembled the Sun, and who possessed it started to have power—power over others.

The creators of wonder tales seem to have recognized the urgency of preserving the wisdom of the balanced Sun-Moon calendar. What better way than to put it into stories with the calendrical rhythm as a backbone? Stories were told and retold, exchanged like goods on the trading routes they knew. People from all over Europe who visited the sacred Megalithic centers would then adapt their own folk's stories to match the new fashion: to tell stories in the calendrical rhythm. Like a new fad, it would be carried home to faraway places along with the latest clay pot or piece of jewelry. It was no superimposed wisdom, rather it was a rhythm people were familiar with anyway, because it was the natural rhythm they lived by. Only later in history, it became the hidden wisdom, which needed to be studied for at least twelve years by bards. At the time of the first Neolithic monuments, the balanced Sun-Moon calendar was something people had lived by for millennia, since it was the natural cosmic cycles as they happened in the sky. As people measured out cycles, and thus created time and calendars to sow and reap, meet and trade, the quality of time became something to experiment with.

Elders watching the development must have been very concerned with reminding the traders and farmers of the old calendar's wisdom. With each tale created according to the balanced calendar, they gave people an intangible "mini-pocket version" of a stone circle calendar to carry with them. What a scheme! Their plan worked, and the soli-lunar calendar became a matrix for the tales of the different folks. The wonder tales contained the wisdom of how humans could walk in awareness and cooperation with the cosmic creation forces, plus they were an instruction on how to dissolve polarities and get back into alignment with the cosmos by reintegrating the lunar quality.

Hands wrapped around my steaming cup of tea, my heart was filled with excitement at this very thought. Even if nobody else was going to acknowledge the connection between the wonder tales and Megalithic monuments, my life had still been transformed for the better in the past few years. I felt that, at least for my personal life, I had found what the renowned astrologer Steven Forrest called "the remedy for the karmic past" when talking about the lunar north node. I had managed to shift my perception back into alignment with the cosmic rhythm through identifying with the wonder tales' heroines. Delving into their philosophies of life, which I came to understand was our Neolithic ancestors' worldview, I managed to retrieve that which had been missing from my life. I was happy (secretly knocking on wood on the table in the café), because I no longer felt painfully bound in a web of lies, codependence, and financial debt. My days were mostly peaceful, as my moods had evened out. In general, anger ceased quicker than it used to and the surges of feeling utterly powerless had become rare. I dared to speak up for myself and even had started to love and accept myself for who I was. But the best thing was that along the road, I had found meaning, a mission, and a higher purpose in life, which helped me find my voice and ultimately write this book. That alone made me feel content and serene. I knew that life was always changing and that I would face new challenges, but also that I had found a way to deal with them—the way of the wonder tales. Now, I knew that bad karmic habits could be changed and their issues dissolved. The bliss I originally experienced during our six-month camping trip triggered the notion of what was missing from my life. Bliss then became my measuring rod, even though the times got tough again afterwards. While sorting out my issues, with the help of wonder tales, I recovered my personal awareness for the lunar quality. In doing so, I did detect some sort of "mechanism to happiness," as I so desperately wished for many years ago on a dark evening around Christmas-time. It turned out to be *the true hero's journey*, the Neolithic balanced soli-lunar calendar, which viewed the north node as the place, where the Sun *and* the Moon's energy equally fused to form a person's fate.

The months before coming to Stonehenge, I had asked myself, if I truly could, in all seriousness, go ahead and claim such theories publicly. Then, I decided to ask an expert. Who else should I ask if not Robin Heath, whose work had provided me with so many answers? When I read this sentence in "Sun, Moon and Stonehenge" I knew he was the one to contact. He wrote:

"Despite all those passing years, the pattern of the past has remained resolutely in place, both in hard stone and in folklore, patiently waiting for its message to be revealed. In due course, the high culture of the past may once again take its rightful place and our story completed."[62]

I reached out to him and he answered with a friendly email. He suggested that I should go ahead and write down my findings. "*Your email suggests that you need to explore and make into a written story an alternative history, based around the Aubrey Circle geometry forming the foundation or basis of Neolithic oral storytelling. I could not disagree that my own work tends to align with your hypothesis.*"

This is what I ended up doing; this is the path I ended up taking at my own *crossroads of destiny*. I followed my hunch to further explore the second, astronomical message of the fairy tales.

62 "Sun, Moon and Stonehenge" by Robin Heath, Bluestone Press 1998, p. 222

Where the Alchemy Happens

I got to meet Robin in person the following summer. His astronomical explanations on a field trip to the Neolithic site of Avebury, near Stonehenge, helped me to use a tale's numerical hints and images, which gave clues that indeed indicated astronomical constellations and real time spans. For example, if the talk in the tale was of "three years of service" then it was in fact three years between one specific constellation and another one marked again by another clue in the story. The entire tale was full of such clues, like *"She comes here every day at twelve and stays about an hour."* This seemed to indicate the rays of the Sun between two markers at a specific time. If I took those hints and images literally, I found that they were describing astronomical positions, and once I got the hang of it, it became like a language that could be read. *Mares* stood for the Moon, their *fouls* for the New Moon, the "holy *Sun*day" was the Sun, and the moment where the protagonist walked through *ninety-nine rooms* was the moment of the *ninety-ninth Full Moon* that occurred in the sky since the story and the cyclical event had begun.

Thus, I was able to set up an entire prototype for the complete lineup of a full aspect circle, from zero degrees to 360 degrees. From there, I could take it further and compare the alignment of many other tales, long or short, and further refine my astrological key sentences. Finally, all fell into its place and I could see the astronomical message in the wonder tales to their full extent. And finally, I had confirmation of something that I had increasingly suspected when researching Neolithic astronomy. It became obvious which part the Neolithic elders ascribed to the lunar north node: They assigned it to the *hero*!

The lunar north node was the protagonist, the human, who walked through life as the focal point of the solar and lunar energies. By being the observer on planet Earth, a human could become aware of being the physical embodiment of their creative energies and thus access the divine. So, *the hero* was a term for a human, who became aware of her collaboration with the divine and learned to co-weave her destiny. And this, our Neolithic ancestors knew and taught in the form of wonder tales.

This must be also what Robin meant in his letter to me:

"Humans who find ways to incorporate the celestial dance and its rhythms into their lives can then and probably only then bring it down to Earth, to manifest it within monuments, temples, and zodiacs and within archetypal stories, musical scales, art works, and certain types of folklore. Drawing heaven down to Earth and marrying the Sun and Moon, are two of the requirements of understanding harmony. The arts that follow on have always been under the Muse."

This is exactly what a protagonist does. Heroines are walking in alignment with the divine. Goals of personal individuation and the heroism popular today are unimportant to them. They strive to integrate *all* the creative energies into their lives and they do not rest until the missing lunar quality is present again and balance is restored. This is when *the alchemy* between humans and the divine can happen, when humans become the representatives of the goddess again.

To be a conscious witness makes the human a dancer to the cosmic tune, an artist, kissed by the muse, who expresses the celestial energies as they fuse through him onto the earthly plane. Everything is connected in one big cosmic plan, one large web of dreams.

Such must have been the wisdom of our Neolithic ancestors. Over the ages, astronomy became separate from astrology, the stone circles were taken apart, and the rocks were used for other purposes. The wonder tales became separate from the stone circles and the balanced calendar was forgotten. Yet, with all the great work of today's archeo-astronomers, archeologists, linguists, and researchers from all different fields of studies, who begin to put the pieces together, there seems to emerge an incredible prehistoric heritage, which lays at our very cultural roots. Our European indigenous wisdom teachings lie hidden in the wonder tales and Megalithic buildings. They are as valid today as 5,000 years ago, showing how the web of dreams is woven. This sacred heritage can provide us with an instruction on how to get back in sync with the divine creative energies. It can help us see the big picture again and return to the awareness that we are all connected to each other and to our environment. The different lens the Neolithic worldview presents can guide us back to a life in balance, peace, and happiness.

Part III

Match the True Hero's Journey to Your Age

The Ancient Wisdom Applied

"A spiritual practice is to be in the right place at the right time."

Robin Heath

In the table of Appendix A, you can look up your age and find the segment and degree of your present cycle. This indicates where you are on your hero's journey. Then you can find explanations of your degree in the corresponding segment chapter and, if you like, compare it to some fairy tale examples.

There can be up to six developmental cycles in a lifetime, each of them is a hero's journey of its own. If a person lives to become 111 years, she will have lived through six journeys. We could also say that she has lived through six wonder tales.

One of the interesting phenomena that showed up in fairy tales and real-life biographies was that some phases seemed to go by with relative ease, and time seemed to move more slowly. Other phases seemed to go by fast. They were more intense and action-packed due to inner and outer turmoil. Therefore, you will notice that the lengths of the segment chapters vary according to the transformational potential they offer. The years that allow you to better align yourself to the cosmic order are, therefore, seemingly more intense and needed lengthier explanations.

The texts in the path segment chapters are my attempt to build a bridge between the old Neolithic wisdom and our modern times. It marks your path to more personal freedom, better relationships, collaboration with your surroundings, more creativity, and peace. In general, one could say it leads to a life kissed by the muse again.

A note to my fellow astrologers: The true hero's journey is indicated by the aspects between the transiting lunar north node and its birth placement.

Some Terms explained

- The **missing quality** means the **missing lunar energy**, which brings skills such as nurturing and care, feminine reproduction and collaboration (to name only a few), all matters of creativity and intuition, into this world.
- The **natural creation process, divine creation process** or **divine workings** are independent of any religious connotation but refer to the mysterious force that creates life on planet Earth in an ongoing process of renewal.
- **Divine creation cycles**, **natural creation cycles**, **creational rhythm**, **carousel of the cycles,** and **divine cosmic order** all mean the same thing: the rhythm of the above-mentioned creation process, which shapes life on Earth, assuming that the interplay between the Sun, the Moon, and the Earth is what creates the world we live in.
- The **elixir** is something life-sustaining, be it of a physical or inspirational nature, that is presented to the heroine at a point of despair.
- The **mission** is a natural consequence of the elixir. It gives the precious incentive the heroine needs to continue her journey and find meaning in it. It mostly has to do with finding ways

to implement the attributes of the missing lunar energy into her own personal life and that of others. In the end, the elixir and the mission always serve to fulfill the soul's higher purpose in life.

- The **higher purpose** is the soul's aim for this lifetime. While the mission can change, the higher purpose always stays the same. It is a potential and, in a way, the higher octave of the mission. It is unchartered territory and can only be pursued when living in a web of dreams.
- I use the terms **spirit** and **the divine** with slightly different connotations. The wonder tales seem to imply that it is the many spirit helpers that assist the heroine in accessing the divine. The divine is the supernatural that stands behind all of creation, while spirit helpers have distinguished functions, each contributing to the creation in their own way.
- A **quantum moment** is a sudden indication in the form of a vision or an inner knowing, which occurs seemingly out of nowhere and illuminates unused potentials. It has to do with the higher purpose of the heroine's soul.
- A **strong lunar influence** occurs when the circle is divided by thirteen, the number of the Moon. I realized that around these degrees the fairy tales always speak of mysterious lunar appearances or moments of strong cyclical pulls.
- **Spinning** and **weaving** always refer to creating destiny.
- The **web of life** expresses the idea that our life is a web, which is constantly being created by how we live our lives. Because everything is interconnected, everything we do always affects

others around us, and thus we contribute to one large collective net, which becomes our social reality. There are two different kinds of webs we can create:

- The **web of dreams** is a destiny created to suit our soul's dreams and desires for peace, love, balance, happiness, and abundance. It leaves us feeling "at home" and builds on virtues of personal integrity, values of benevolence and collaboration, and respect for all beings. By consciously attuning to the flow of the divine creation cycles, people naturally produce a web of dreams.
- The **web of lies** is a destiny created to suit the ego's wish for status, possessions, and individuality at the expense of others. It builds on values of self-centeredness, survival of the fittest, competition, and lack of consideration, but in the end, it leaves us feeling alienated and cut off.
- **New future** and **new era** are used to express that the web of life now changes from a web of lies to a web of dreams.
- **Shadow forces** are inner and outer "ghosts" from the past, remnants of wrongdoings, wrong timings, and the consequence of a web of lies. They need to be faced bravely by focusing on the mission and the soul's higher purpose. It asks for the virtues and values of the web of dreams. Then they will have no foundation and will dissolve along the journey, as the heroine moves in the flow of the cosmic cycles.
- The **crossroads of destiny** are two points, when the heroine must make major decisions on her journey, which are going to alter the course of her destiny.

These are the fairy tale examples I used as examples:

"The Twelve Wild Ducks," Norway

"The Girl Without Hands," Germany (Grimm)

"Hansel and Gretel," Germany (Grimm)

"The Sun-Horse," Slovakia

"All-Kinds-of-Fur," Germany (Grimm)

"The Princess in the Cavern," Sweden

"Hans in Luck," Germany (Grimm)

"Iliane, who Commands the Flowers," Romania

"Sleeping Beauty," Germany (Grimm)

"Rumpelstiltskin," Germany (Grimm)

"Wassilissa the Beautiful," Russia

"Lilla Rosa and Long Leda," Sweden

The First Segment of the Cycle

0 degrees to 51.42 degrees

Discovering that Something is Missing

Realizing that there is an imbalance in life
and that it is somehow incomplete.
Getting a vision of how powerful it could be if it were complete.

Each new hero's journey starts with a sense of incompleteness. A deep longing for a reality where the lunar energy and all that it stands for (creativity, rhythm, nurturing, caring, intuition, benevolence, collaboration, to name only a few) is fully present. It causes the heroine to go look for that which is missing in life. She senses that this missing quality would make life so much more happy, balanced, and rich.

As this new cycle begins, the heroine starts to look for values of integrity, which she feels will complete her life and bring peace and harmony. This attitude triggers new visions and opens a door to new choices, which promise quick fixes. This is not the solution yet, but it is a step in the right direction and activates help from the spiritual side of life. A collaboration with the destiny-shaping forces starts once the heroine listens to her heart and follows her intuition. At one point, the realization sets in of what it is that has been missing all along, and the intent to go retrieve it grows, especially when a sudden inkling releases a feeling of omnipotence. It is an inspiration of how life could feel if it were complete. There would be so much more creative energy at the heroine's disposal, and life would be so much easier, full of beauty, love, and recognition. It is such a powerful experience that initially drives the sensible human to go looking for that which is missing, hoping to make it an everyday reality of life. This initial jolt of omnipotence is initially no more than uncontrollable potential; it will need to mature over time into a steady flow of energy, which will be experienced at every given moment. At this point the creative energy cannot really be handled yet and needs training and refinement, like a craft that needs to be learned from the bottom up to be used properly. However, it gives a hint of what will be possible in the future despite the difficulties that will inevitably arise once on the journey. It entices the heroine to recover the missing lunar energy and move into alignment with the cosmic order, which holds the promise of balance, peace, and abundance.

The Aspects of the First Segment

Zero degrees (strong lunar influence): Life is incomplete, a notion that triggers an in-limbo state, resulting in feelings of isolation and separation.

You notice an imbalance in your life. It is as if something vital were missing. Instead of peace and abundance, there is conflict and scarcity; instead of flow and a sense of renewal, there is stagnation. A deep longing for a different reality starts to set in. The wish for more creativity, more love, more balance, and for values of integrity and goodwill sets in. What happened? Where did the ease and joy in life go? For a sensitive person such as you, the imbalance becomes unbearable at this point, and you feel called to do something about it. It is here that your road to mastery starts.

6 degrees: A vision of a complete reality is harbored.

The feeling that something is missing from your life and a subtle idea of how things could be if life were complete increase your willingness to listen to your intuition. This again strengthens the reconnection to the suppressed or missing lunar energy in your life. A vision is triggered, and new possibilities are seen that let you break out of your regular thinking patterns.

12.86 degrees: New opportunities come up. They offer to make this vision a reality.

The opportunity to act differently than in the past arises. It requires courage to listen to your inner guidance and act accordingly. It is time to shake up the status quo. If you follow your intuition and do what needs to be done, especially if it means breaking out of your regular frame of acting, things are going in the right direction and you are taking your first step on your journey.

Fairy tale examples:

- A queen had a nose bleed, and as she saw the blood on the snow, she started to think that she had twelve sons and no daughters *(the unbalanced Sun–Moon ratio)* and realized how much she longed for a daughter. For the first time, she spoke her thoughts aloud and said that she wouldn't care what became of her sons, if only she had a daughter.

- A man had lost all his money. All he had left was a mill and an apple tree *(all he would need to create a happy life)* behind the house. But one day, a man in green *(the devil)* came up to him and made him an offer.
- There was a couple that did not have enough food to feed their children. They decided to leave their children with the last piece of bread in the woods. The boy Hansel heard this and put bright pebbles *(that shimmered in the light of the Moon)* into his pocket to guide them home.

18 degrees: Destiny's gate stands wide open and calls the human to go change what desperately needs to be changed. The hope for a quick fix is enticing.

The gate to a new destiny stands wide open and calls you to walk through it. You might think that the rash solution you now see fixes all your problems immediately. While it might do so temporarily, there will be more work awaiting you in the matter. However, for now it is a good thing to walk through that gate and be confident and hopeful.

25.71 degrees (strong lunar influence): A glance at the missing quality is given. What may have been dormant due to social conditionings is being re-awoken.

What was suppressed due to social restraints is becoming more evident, and you get an idea of what could be missing from your life. A chance presents itself to reawaken abilities that were inactive due to social restraints. A quantum moment—like a sudden inner knowing or some kind of "aha!"—happens. This impulse has a strong lunar imprint and comes from beyond regular thinking patterns. It comes from the spirit realm and has a broadening effect on your mind.

30 degrees: With the recognition of completeness also comes the sudden awareness of what has been missing all along.

With the quantum moment, which was a sudden indication of how life could be if the lunar energy were included in daily reality, also comes the realization of what has been missing from your life all along. You get an idea of what it is you're lacking. It is not too pleasant of a time, since putting your finger on what is not there lets you realize that the glass is half empty.

Fairy tale examples:

- The queen would exchange her twelve sons for a single daughter. An old troll witch *(incorporating the lunar energy)* appears and promises her a daughter. The condition is that the witch will take her boys once the girl is christened. *(The queen must choose between the two calendars. As we have seen, Christianity favors the solar calendar. If she therefore were to live by the old balanced solar-lunar calendar and not christen her daughter, the Moon, she would be able to keep all her children.)*

- The king led the sun-horse up and down to provide his kingdom with light, otherwise it would all be dark. Where he went with his sun-horse, a light shone as if it were the brightest day, but when the horse was gone, the darkest of nights rolled over the land. *(Both Sun and Moon are missing.)*
- The king had to promise his wife on her deathbed that he would only marry a woman with hair as golden as hers *(a woman with the lunar quality)*. However, no bride could be found as pretty as his dead queen. *(So the lunar energy went missing in the kingdom.)*

36 degrees: A surge of optimism and a feeling of omnipotence entice the human to move on.

A rush of powerful inspiration now drives you to change things in your life. The envisioned completeness triggers the feeling that things are possible, and you are confident that obstacles can be overcome, no matter their size. Maybe you feel like you are on a crusade, full of courage and confidence. This feeling holds the promise of how things could be in the future, once the boundaries and restrictions to creative expression are torn down.

40 degrees: Mostly unnoticed, the potential for completeness is growing.

Room is made on the inside for new qualities to grow, which eventually will make life complete and balanced. The growth still takes place hidden from plain view, like in pregnancy, but things are beginning to change for the better. A seed is sown, so to speak, and now grows under divine protection.

45 degrees: The hope for a new future triggers the impulse to move on, but at the same time, old patterns are pulling back.

Now the impact of the missing becomes evident everywhere in life. How could you have been so blind or so ignorant? The search for the missing lunar energy intensifies and evokes adversaries. The hope for a better future urges you to move on, but at the same time, old patterns are pulling back. Society knows you in a certain way and it seems not to want to see you change. Why shake up the status quo? You might be asking this, but still you *must* do it. You *must* search for new ways, even if it means that you are clashing with other positions and opinions. Resistance against your endeavors might be forming, and you are no longer the people pleaser that you might once have been. As much as you'd like to, there is no turning back to the old ways. You meet nothing but resistance from yourself and from society, which is used to suppress all lunar energy. If you want more care, more love, more harmony and creativity, the world around you and parts of yourself are trying to prove that this will not be possible. It helps to reconnect to the lunar energy from time-to-time and not forget that you are well on the road to restoring it back into your life.

Fairy tale examples:

- The queen gave birth to a daughter, just like the troll witch had promised. For a moment the queen's life was complete—twelve sons and one daughter *(the balanced soli-lunar calendar*—but as soon as her daughter was christened, her sons were turned into wild ducks and flew off.

- One day, the sun-horse was stolen, and from then on, the land was in complete darkness. The wish grew urgent to find the light. People in the kingdom became unhappy and scared, and their king was in great distress.
- The prince took the finely woven handkerchief of his beloved, promising that he would never forget her *(the lunar princess)*, and then they had to part. The princess was brought into a cave, and the prince went to defend the land at her father's side. Luck was not on their side, however, and the old king died. The young prince had to flee back to his homeland, and the enemy took over the land.

The issue in all three tales is not yet resolved. Bigger changes than those already made are necessary to restore balance, (Sun and Moon-) light and peace.

The Second Segment of the Cycle

51.42 degrees to 102.85 degrees

Getting to Know the Missing Energy

**Becoming more familiar with the lunar energy,
which in essence is what is truly missing.
Learning not to fear it and leaving the old ways behind.**

For the lunar energy to be re-integrated, the old ways will have to be abandoned soon, since they favor the suppression of the lunar energy. But first the missing quality needs to be contacted and its subtle impulses noticed and trusted. If the heroine starts to get a sense of the missing lunar quality and does not react in fear when it appears, mistaking it for something evil, she will now be equipped to recover it. This happens best when a connection is established, where the mind enters the spirit realm and seeks to find advice and a connection to the divine inner source. New and creative ways are found to deal with the surroundings and society. It becomes evident what is helpful in recovering the missing quality and what is blocking it. By discerning the helpful from the preventing, the connection to the missing quality can be further strengthened and a protective sphere is provided to do so.

Reality can be explored with this new awareness, and consequentially, something life-changing begins to form. As the heroine reaches out and responds to it, a connection can be made, and the journey is under divine protection from now on. Things are no longer as they once were, and it is time to let go of the old roles and behaviors. Masks are falling. To look at things in the old way becomes dangerous. A threshold is being crossed.

The Aspects of the Second Segment

51.42 degrees: Support is given to advance matters. Depending on the degree of incompleteness, the missing quality can be perceived for what it truly is, or it is mistaken for something dangerous, evil or ugly.

By establishing a connection to the spirit realm, you can subtly begin to grasp the quality of the lunar energy and what it could bring to your life. In a moment of communication, be it in a dream or other open-minded state, your consciousness is reminded of your soul's higher purpose. It might be revealed in a moment of sudden recognition yet giving you no more than a quick glimpse of a future potential. Since the frame for it is not yet established, its consequences cannot be fully understood. You might only fully understand this piece of information in hindsight. However, here you get a glimpse of your soul's higher purpose. So, whatever it is you grasp now is dear to you, and you will not forget it so easily again.

55 degrees (strong lunar influence): Becoming equipped to recover the missing quality.

If you are attentive during this time, you will receive a tool or spirit guide that will support you on your quest.

60 degrees: Getting to know the surroundings. Something potentially life changing is beginning to take shape.

Equipped with a growing understanding of the lunar quality and a tool or helper that can guide you, you start to explore your surroundings from a different angle. You see familiar things in a completely new way and meet new things in your life with curiosity. Reality explored with this new awareness will bring something your way with the potential to alter the course of your life.

72 degrees: New and creative ways of interacting with the surroundings.

Talents you never dreamed of can now start to unfold. Your creative abilities to shape the physical world want to be expressed and explored. You are finding a new way of interacting with your environment, and you want to shine your light and make a difference. It becomes evident what is helpful in recovering the missing quality and what is blocking the process.

Fairy tale examples:

- The queen's only daughter grows up without her twelve brothers, but she is often sad and withdrawn. One day, the queen tells her that her brothers have become wild ducks. The girl now feels drawn to go search for them. On her long way through endless forests, she dreams of the path that will lead her to their house. *(Due to her dream, she is equipped to proceed on her quest.)*

- Hans trades in his lump of gold for a horse. He got exactly what he wished for and feels rightfully confirmed by destiny. He looks at the world from a new perspective now, from the back of a horse. Feeling lighter and equipped to travel faster, he tests out the horse and clicks his tongue. *(He feels very exhilarated that he can move lighter and faster now.)*
- The king looking for the sun-horse finds the faint light of the morning sun behind a thousand woods. There is a little house and inside is a seer who agrees to find the sun-horse for him. The seer travels a long distance until he comes to the realm of a witch and her daughters. *(He enters the realm where the cycles are made.)* To spy on them, he transforms himself into a bird.

75 degrees: Careful discernment is required.

You absolutely need to discern the helpful from that which prevents you from being successful. What is holding you back? What serves you and what doesn't? By discerning the conducive from the restraining, you determine what is strengthening your connection to the lunar quality and what is not. Since this quest is about thinking differently and going down new roads, you always need to recollect what it is you want and what goal you're after. At this point, you could easily get distracted by your newfound creativity or your musings to give the physical world a new shape. The shadows lie where you do not take responsibility for yourself and your actions.

80 degrees: A protective sphere is provided to further strengthen the connection to the missing quality.

If you do take responsibility for yourself as you continue a quest with an ever-growing awareness, you enter a mysterious protective sphere, where the divine will hold a shielding hand over you. As you reach out and act from your heart, the divine responds and offers you protection on your journey. It serves to let you further explore and kindle your relationship with the lunar energy.

90 degrees: A threshold is crossed. The old must now be left behind.

Things become tense around you. Masks are falling. To look at things in the old way becomes dangerous. You are crossing a threshold. You must say goodbye to the old role you used to play. Now you see clearly the real face of the people around you, and you see clearly through situations. Make good use of this new viewpoint; it is a gift.

Fairy tale examples:

- The girl entered the hut she had seen in her dream and found twelve chairs and twelve beds, recognizing them as her twelve brothers'. She hid underneath the bed, and the door opened. In flew twelve wild ducks that changed into princes as they crossed over the threshold. *(She is now witnessing life from her new viewpoint at the threshold between the two worlds, the tangible and the intangible realms.)*

- The young man in search of Iliane received a copper bridle from holy Monday *(the Moon's spirit helper)*. As soon as he shook it, a copper horse appeared. He mounted, and as fast as a thought was at the house of holy Friday; maybe she knew. *(This is certainly a hint at the Nordic goddess Freya).*
- The princess took the spindle and wondered: "What thing is this that twists round so briskly?" As soon as she touched it, the evil prophecy was fulfilled, she pricked her finger with it and fell back upon the bed that stood there. She lay in a deep sleep and this sleep fell upon the whole castle . . . *(This scene perfectly shows how Sleeping Beauty tries to discern what a spindle/cycle is. She has never heard of it, because her parents tried to keep it from her. Therefore, she has no way of discerning for herself; nevertheless, the goddess puts her into the protective sphere of a deep sleep. This is the threshold she crosses, and with her, the entire castle falls asleep.)*

The Third Segment of the Cycle

102.85 degrees to 154.28 degrees

Finding the Elixir and a Mission

Something important is found or given that sustains the soul in difficult times and reminds her of the mission. A personal transformational process is triggered as the formerly missing lunar energy is retrieved and attunement to the cosmic cycles takes place.

This third segment starts at a point of crisis. The heroine has just crossed over a threshold into a different mental state, where all around her suddenly the masks are falling, and she sees what is behind. This isolates her from the world. She feels lonely and separate. It is a troublesome time full of struggle, but it serves to heighten her awareness of the lunar energy. She needs to find stability within herself, which is best achieved by turning inward and connecting to the inner spiritual guidance. This prepares the ground for something unusual to happen. As she finds her inner well, direct access to the divine, she is given a glimpse of the higher purpose of her quest. In the middle of feeling abandoned and isolated, a life-sustaining elixir is either given or found. It marks the beginning of the collaboration between the heroine and the divine. The heroine becomes inspired by the elixir and takes on the task of re-introducing the divine lunar energy into human awareness, which is from now on going to be her mission. Once the mission is taken on, re-alignment with the natural creation cycles is prepared. Being attuned to the cycles, and therefore being in the right place at the right time, is a prerequisite for the fulfillment of the mission.

As the alignment happens, the tremendous power of the divine creation process is experienced. It can be quite overwhelming for the heroine. All focus must stay on the mission in order not to abandon the alignment. Clear determination is therefore of the utmost importance at this point. If all goes well, fast speed towards fulfillment of the mission will set in.

The Aspects of the Third Segment

102.85 degrees: Struggle and isolation make the missing quality painfully evident. Yet it is here where reconnection to the missing can be permanently established.

It is not an easy time for you right now. You might feel isolated and lonely, since you are in a very different state of mind than the world around you. You might even see behind things and get spiritual insights you otherwise don't. What is most important now, however, is that you strengthen your connection to spirit. Turn inward and reconnect to the divine within you. It is a source of help and inspiration in these times of struggle and maybe even darkness. You cannot see it now, but it serves you to heighten your awareness of the missing in your life. Your pain makes you aware of it, and this again helps you access the missing lunar quality. It is almost as if you could befriend it now. But be aware; this process might provoke old shadows from the past to come up. As you try to sort them out and make sense of them, try not to be overcome by fear. The oblivion of the lunar energy in your environment might already be so deeply rooted that you are up against a lot of resistance. This might confuse you, but just stick to your innate well of wisdom. Spirit is supporting you from the inside; do not despair.

105 degrees: Preparation for something unusual to happen.

This time of isolation and inward turning is preparing you for important things to happen soon. Your soul nudges you to keep moving toward your higher purpose. It is only a subtle feeling that draws your attention in a new direction, but it is something very dear and familiar to your heart. It's kind of like a sweet spot that is attracting you.

108 degrees (strong lunar influence): A life-sustaining elixir is found or given. It sets free a before-unknown inner strength, which stems from the growing connection to the formerly missing quality.

It is an intense time, and in the middle of it, you receive or are led to find a life-sustaining elixir. The elixir is something that nurtures you in this time of struggle. It can be a new kind of experience, a new tool to master your difficulties, a newly discovered talent or a gift. In any case, it is something that supplies you with hope, inspiration and a new vision. Suddenly you understand what kind of light your soul could shine, if you would only let it. There is so much potential, so many goals and high aims, which are all obstructed and constrained by the overlay of a society that denies the presence of a major creative participant, the Moon. If there were no constraints, your soul could shine her light, always share its wisdom, and live out its connection to the divine. It could co-create life side-by-side with the divine and leave a positive mark on this world. This elixir moment sets free a before-unknown inner strength, which stems from your growing connection to the lunar energy. In all of this, your mission is born. But only when you have received what you so badly needed to nourish your physical body can your soul start to think of her mission.

Fairy tale examples:

- Hansel was put in a cage *(isolation)* and Gretel had to cook food for him. *(The ground for something unusual is prepared).* "And now the best food was cooked for poor Hansel," the tale says. *(This is his elixir—to be nourished so that he will not starve to death but come back to life to fulfill his soul's mission.)*
- In a year's time the young queen had a baby and thought no more of the little man. But one day he came suddenly into her room, and said, "Now give me what you promised me." The queen was terrified and offered the little man all the riches of the kingdom if he would only leave the child, but the little man said, "No, I would rather have something living than all the treasures of the world." Then the queen began to weep, so that the little man had pity. "I will give you three days," said he, "and if at the end of that time you cannot tell my name, you must give up the child to me." *(The queen is given the elixir of time. If Rumpelstiltskin were really such a bad creature, he would have taken her baby right away. But*

he rather wants her to remember his name—the name of the goddess.[63] *Even though it seems to be in a negative context to our modern understanding, this moment of elixir sends her on a mission to find out the goddess's name, which again will lead her to the balanced calendar and the chance for a happier life.)*

- Roses grew around the castle *(protecting Sleeping Beauty in her isolation)* and nobody could go through. One day, a young prince came, and the hedge of thorns turned into nice flowers and he could pass easily. *(The ground is prepared for something unusual to happen.)* He found Sleeping Beauty and awakened her with a kiss. *(They are each other's elixir. They represent the sacred couple of the Sun and the Moon.)*

115 degrees: New hope is gained, and again, careful discernment is required.

A new direction appears on your quest, and you find new drive to move on. However, you will want to act from a place of newfound inner power and knowing and therefore carefully discern each situation.

120 degrees: The promise of fulfillment can be felt, which now drives forward.

With increased enthusiasm, you move on with your life. The promise for a happier future lies in the air; just do not stay passive or lethargic. You feel how the creative energy wants to connect your heart with the mind. Are you serious about re-integrating the lunar energy

63 See "Beauty and the Beast" in Appendix B, where the beast is the goddess

into your daily life and are you letting your soul nudge you in a more fulfilling direction?

130 degrees: Arriving at destiny's crossroads. It is a turning point, the result of former efforts.

This crossroads holds the promise to purposefully reshape your fate if the newfound quality can be upheld and carried on. So the questions are: Are you willing to restore balance in your life and are you willing to take the lunar energy fully into account from now on? As you arrive at destiny's crossroads, you therefore must ask yourself: Is the formerly missing quality now acknowledged? This will allow your mission to be carried out.

Fairy tale examples:

- The sister who found her twelve brothers as wild ducks offered to free them from their enchantment, if they only let her live. *(She is their elixir, and they hers, as the Sun–Moon relationship goes).* They all found new hope in her promise, and the brothers spared her life *(this marks the crossroads of destiny).*
- The princess was given the advice to go find employment at the palace. With new hope, she continued her journey and soon came to a large body of water *(destiny's crossroads).*
- Hansel stretched out a little bone and the witch thought it was his finger, puzzled that he did not gain weight. *(New hope is gained and promises a better future.)* One day, she wanted to roast him anyway *(arriving at destiny's crossroads).*

135 degrees: The opportunity to purposefully reshape fate comes with the requirement to think and act differently.

You must courageously face the intensifying energies since the process will also provoke the surfacing of shadows. Still, the imbalanced past wants to hold you back. At the same time, preparation is going on for full re-alignment with the natural creation cycles. You sense this, and it gives you the necessary zest to confront that which needs to be confronted and to continuously move in the direction your heart and soul desire. Therefore, an inner drive mobilizes you to overcome all obstacles, and your intention to be in the right place at the right time is high. You need to adjust your way of thinking and acting, however.

144 degrees (strong lunar influence): A relapse to the past can and must be avoided now if the right effort is made. Calm inward focus helps to be clearly determined and not fall back into old habits.

Finally, the chains of the past can be broken. The fairy tales show that the attunement of the heroine with the cosmic cycles happens at this point. It is the moment when the missing lunar energy is recovered, and a kind of a bridge is erected, which allows for the tremendous power of the divine to re-enter the awareness of the heroine. It is this complete carousel of natural creative energies that eventually will bring balance. Yet now, you might be feeling only the dizzying upheavals and distress to stay on track, and all outside forces seem to be pulling you away. In this moment of alignment to the full range of cosmic energy, you get to experience the tremendous power of the divine creation energy. It can be quite overwhelming, and it is not easy to handle these intensifying energies. Since it does emanate a strong power, it might seem to you as demonic or having bad intentions, but this energy only reflects what was suppressed before. However, notice that you also feel a tremendous power surge. Don't fear it; this is also not demonic. If you give into fear and selfish reactions, havoc will be wreaked. What you need is calm and determined focus, since now is the moment to avoid falling back into old patterns! If you manage to hold on to your vision with clear intent, things will never be the same from now on. The process to recover the missing lunar quality is in full progress, and this is a moment of vital importance.

150 degrees: Tensions are high and growth is happening quickly. No matter what is being done, whether actions and reactions happen out of trust or fear, they amplify the inner attitude.

Your alignment with the divine creation cycles should have been successful, and now you are riding the carousel of the creational rhythm. Or in other words, you are now in the flow and things should get easier. However, it is a time of work and service to the greater whole. You will find security in bundling your energies and making sense of what has happened to you so far. The full power spectrum of creative energies is at your disposal now and naturally empowers your mission. Carefully re-check from time to time your visions so you stay on track.

Fairy tale examples:

- After the twelve brothers spared the life of their sister, they instructed her about what she needs to do to free them from their enchantment. She needs to pick thistledown, card it, spin it, and weave it; and make twelve coats. And while she does that, she is not allowed to talk, laugh, or weep. *(This chore will align the princess to the spinning and weaving motion of the natural cycles. She is not allowed to react on emotions—old habits—but needs to fully concentrate on her mission to save her brothers.)*

- Suddenly the wood became full of a terrible noise and the Baba Yaga came flying. She was riding in a great iron mortar and commanded her little house to turn around, stand still, and open. *(The turning of the house is a hint to the cycles and their alignment to who wants to get "in." Therefore she commands the cycles.)* She smelled Wassilissa, who was sent to borrow fire. The old witch agreed to give her fire if Wassilissa worked for her. "If not, thou shalt be eaten for my supper." *(The fire of life and renewal cannot just be fetched without doing something in exchange. Otherwise it will consume humans. This means that Wassilissa needs to get to know the divine workings within the cycles of creation.)*
- Gretel was ordered to make fire in the oven to roast Hansel. *(The oven is a motherly symbol. It is the place where old is burned to be made new, like a cremation fire.)* Gretel managed to shove the witch into the oven, where she burned to death. *(It is an intense moment, where Gretel comes very close to the divine renewal cycle. Quickly she must decide whether she wants to live or die.)*

The Fourth Segment of the Cycle

154.28 degrees to 205.42 degrees

Attuning to the Cosmic Order

As the lunar quality is retrieved and the alignment with the cosmic order in place, the lunar quality needs to be re-introduced into society. This may expose imbalances.

The heroine's reality is changing. As things swing back into balance, shadow forces are dissolved, and all falls back into its rightful place. The ground for completeness is laid and its wisdom needs to be applied. Then the possibility of a life in balance and harmony is given. Instead of war, there will be peace; instead of scarcity and stagnation, there will be healthy renewal.

Even though the missing quality is fully recovered by now, it still needs to be re-introduced into society and find broad acknowledgement. Only then will the balance be complete inside and out. Once this is the case, healthy and ongoing renewal can take place and the unnamable feelings of longing will dissolve. Instead, fulfillment and happiness will become the rule.

As much as power or ground has been gained, at this point there are still further tasks waiting. They will serve to also re-introduce the recovered quality into a larger context, into society and the personal surroundings. This happens in the form of carrying out the personal mission. There is much idealism and a strong will to push forward; however, potential dangers smolder. They stem from unresolved shadow forces and must be considered and faced, as they will inevitably surface sooner or later. To bring them to light, a testing phase will expose the level of integrity. To what degree can the recovered energy already be worked with? Where are there still inadequacies?

The Aspects of the Fourth Segment

154.28 degrees: Direct exposure to the mysterious, transcending forces at work. It serves to experience their vast power and become familiar with their laws.

You are mostly freed from the past now, which opens you up to new experiences. As things swing into a new balance, shadow forces are dissolving, and your reality starts to change. As you get direct exposure to the divine creation energies, you meet their tremendous power and realize that you are on the verge of stepping into a new kind of power.

160 degrees: Witnessing the divine workings. The potential of a wholesome life is unfolding. The opportunity presents itself to contribute to a more balanced human reality.

For the new power, which comes from alignment with the cosmic cycles, to unfold within you, you get a chance to witness the divine workings. This means that you might have dreams or sudden deep insights into things, which you did not even consider before. A collaboration with the divine to reach completeness becomes possible. Suddenly you begin to get ideas about "what makes the world go around," and you get an idea about the part you want to play in it. This is when your higher purpose starts to shine through again. It is your soul's nudging to participate in the cycles of creation. It might feel a little frightening and fill you with awe, because you are treading on holy ground. Ideally, at some point, a deep inner trust will well up inside, and you will feel inspired to get to work and find out more.

Fairy tale examples:

- Baba Yaga turned to the gate and shouted: "Ho! Ye, my solid locks, unlock! Thou, my stout gate, open!" The locks unlocked instantly, the gate opened of itself, Wassilissa entered behind her and immediately the gate shut again, and the locks snapped tight. *(Now they are in the realm of the goddess where the cycles are made.)* Wassilissa wondered at finding the hut filled with such an abundance of everything. From now on, she had to cook and do all sorts of chores for Baba Yaga. *(The girl got to enter the divine realm and witness the divine workings—for example, the changing of day and night— and she had to help the goddess with seasonal work, just like Golden Mary at Mother Holle's.)*
- Gretel now ran to Hansel and freed him. He sprang like a bird from its cage and they rejoiced that they were safe. They went into the witch's house and saw in every corner chests

full of pearls and jewels. *(They also find abundance in the goddess's house.)* They filled their pockets and left to go home.

- Every day the sister tended the house for her twelve brothers, who came home in the evenings and changed from wild ducks into princes. The last day, the girl was out plucking thistledown and a prince rode by and saw her. *(He witnesses her divine working as she plucked and spun a new destiny for her brothers.)* He asked her name, but she didn't answer. He liked her so much that he wanted to take her to his castle and marry her.

165 degrees (strong lunar influence): Fulfillment draws near.

By attuning to the natural creative cycles, you have come far and reached a solid foundation for peace, love, and happiness. Balance is mostly re-established in your life, and it only needs to be maintained from now on. This means that your insights about the natural creative cycles and how to reach completeness always want to be applied from now on. You sense what it means to be of service to the divine in always creating a life in harmony. As the prerequisites to fulfill your mission are set up, the upcoming second half of your journey will be about implementing what you learned into your environment. You know that you are not an island and that the peace and creativity you are emanating now is affecting other people as well, wanting to be extended and shared. Support will be provided by Spirit.

There is another notion coming up, as an unusual opportunity occurs during this time. It shows you that your soul longs to go up to an even higher octave and move even further into unchartered territory. It longs to fulfill an even higher purpose. What it is can still not really be told, but as you have already subtly felt from time-to-time, there is an inner longing that pulls you in a new direction. Whatever that notion, you might want to give in and see where it leads you. It is certainly worth the exploration. The opportunity that presents itself to you now will let you contribute to a balanced life beyond the scope of your own and your immediate surroundings.

180 degrees: Manifestation and acknowledgement of the new status by the environment. Power is gained or lost again.

The reward of your empowerment process is about to be presented. It is a moment of recognition. However, depending on the degree of suppression of the lunar energy in your environment, the balanced inner power you emanate now stirs resistance in your surroundings. If they do not want to have the lunar energy resurface—because of, for example, not wanting to let go of conveniences, old patterns, or false securities—they will start trying to take your power away and pull you back into your old status. It might get difficult again. If you let your unbalanced environment pull you away from your balanced status, however, you'll start to forget about the lunar energies again and eventually lose your attunement to the cycles, falling back into a state of imbalance. It is not always easy to stay in balance when facing an environment that rejects the lunar energies.

However, keep in mind that in our time and age, the new status of completeness is seldom fully acknowledged right away, and there are further tasks awaiting you as presented in many longer tales. You have recovered the missing lunar energy in your life and gained balance and power through it; now it is your task to re-introduce it to the society you live in. It is a kind of service to your surroundings. Only then will the achieved balance be complete inside and out and will you be acknowledged for it, just as you acknowledge others. You, therefore, must help re-introduce the recovered lunar energy into a larger context. Once this is the case, healthy and ongoing renewal will take place for all to enjoy. It will mean peace, happiness, and abundance for all.

195 degrees (strong lunar influence): Potential dangers from unresolved shadow forces need to be taken into account.

You have strong determination to help implement the achieved balance into your surroundings. But since people might not have exactly waited for you to do so, they are possibly reacting with a good deal of resistance. Some might even react outright defensively, because it brings their shadow issues to light. Your mission helps you to stay on track though. You have much idealism, but you need to consider potential dangers from those unresolved shadow issues in your environment. They will inevitably surface, since they are a natural side effect of the imbalance and suppressed lunar energy.

200 degrees: A testing phase now exposes the level of integrity in the human's environment.

How complete and balanced is your environment? To what degree can the recovered lunar energy already be worked with? How do people react to your request for integrity and awareness? Are people aware of all the energies that make up the natural creation process or is the lunar energy still suppressed? Is the system open for renewal or is it functioning on a web of lies? You might be pushed into the position of having to defend yourself and holding your values up high. This time also tests you and your virtues. Is your personal integrity well-rooted and are you living the web of dreams that enables your soul to follow her purpose? Can you withstand the pressure from outside or do you succumb? In any case, it brings the remaining shadow forces to light and shows how balanced or imbalanced the system you live in is.

In this test of integrity, it helps to be in intense communication with spirit. It guides you on how to react and where there is more work to do. Your soul knows that it can only live out her higher purpose when continually creating a web of dreams, a life co-created from a position of balance and completeness in attunement with the divine.

Fairy tale examples:

- Wassilissa received help for the many tasks she had to do for Baba Yaga from her little doll, which her mother had given her on her deathbed *(help from spirit/the ancestors)*. After a meal, Baba Yaga said to her, "Well, why dost thou say nothing, but stand there as if thou wast dumb?" *(For the first time, Wassilissa is acknowledged as a presence in the room.)* "I spoke not," Wassilissa answered, "because I dared not. But if thou wilt allow me, grandmother, I wish to ask thee some questions." *(She is determined to find out more.)* "Well," said the old witch, "only remember that every question does not lead to good. If thou knowest overmuch, thou wilt grow old too soon. What wilt thou ask?" Wassilissa now asked three questions about the mysterious events that were taking place in the goddess's realm. *(She senses that there is potential danger if she asks further questions. This tale demonstrates a test of integrity between the goddess and a human. In a way, it is always this kind of inner dispute that goes on in the testing phase and has a lot to do with asking yourself what is right and what is wrong.)*

- The prince fell in love with Rosa and asked her to marry him. They sailed away from the lonely island, where Rosa had been a castaway, and took with them the budding linden tree to plant in her new home's garden. In it sang the nightingale and awoke great joy in the surroundings. A while after their wedding, she gave birth to a son and informed her father but did not tell him of the evil deeds of her stepmother. *(The tale does not end here, because for the next generation to grow up in balance, Rosa still must deal with the shadow force in the shape of her evil stepmother, who represents the imbalance of her society. Rosa staying quiet about the misdeeds of her stepmother is not an act of integrity. The tale demonstrates that it leaves room for the shadow forces to harm her again.)*
- The girl took off her furs, washed the soot from her face, opened the nutshell and took out her dress that shone as bright as the Sun. She put it on and went up to the ball. She was so beautiful that everyone thought she was a princess. The king came, gave her his hand, and they danced together all night long. When the dance ended, she was gone, and nobody knew where she had gone. She rushed back to the kitchen, put the furs back on and made her face dirty again

so that she was again All-kinds-of-Fur. She now had to cook a soup for the king, but not to let a hair fall in. *(I assume this meant her golden hair, which would stand for the golden aura she has as a representative of the goddess. The cook is afraid of what would happen if the king found the lunar energy present at his court.)*

The Fifth Segment of the Cycle

205.42 degrees to 257.08 degrees

Anchoring the New Reality

A transformational process is triggered in the heroine's surroundings due to the return of the formerly missing lunar energy.

The testing phase is not quite over yet. The more the power of the gained understanding manifests within the heroine, the more the outside world reacts to it. The heroine's power is directly mirrored with an increased activity of the shadow forces. As their effects can now be clearly witnessed and pointed out by the heroine, it is important that she now firmly stands her ground. She needs to hold onto her personal level of integrity and let herself be guided by Spirit as things become uncomfortable. Shadows do not like to be exposed. The heroine might even have to resort to some wise maneuvers or a shamanic kind of trickery when it gets to the point where her surroundings seem to absolutely misunderstand or deny her power. Based on all that has been learned so far, she can come to the right conclusions and make the decisions that are attuned to the cosmic cycles. If she does not, her personal identity might be in danger and she could lose herself.

From all this pure intention, an energetic bridge is erected, allowing yet for another transformational process. It becomes possible for the heroine to cross over into a more complete and balanced life, where the mission can finally find accomplishment. Things are starting to fall into their proper place, and final redemption from shadow forces starts to take place.

The Aspects of the Fifth Segment

205.42 degrees: The extent of the newly gained power becomes evident and is mirrored by increased resistance from the environment.

As the test of integrity continues a little while longer, the tension increases for you. The shadow forces gain strength. Even though you might be angry and disappointed by the reactions of your surroundings, you must firmly stand your ground and not let yourself be fooled by the shady offers you might get. Your adversaries are not as harmless as they pretend. They have a lot to lose, be it their status or their financial benefits. Their power is based on profits gained in a solar-only focused patriarchal system. Your newly gained quality of life, which includes the lunar energy, threatens them. You can now witness the shadow forces at work. It is important that you stick to your values and not let yourself be bought or tricked out of your newfound balanced identity. When necessary, become the wise trickster who anticipates the moves of your adversaries and beats them with their own weapons. The difference between the two of you is that you act with the highest good of everyone's soul in mind, while they only think of their own profit. This makes them susceptible to trickery because it is the language they speak. However, if you do not feel suited to be the sacred trickster, you may also just show no emotion and continue to do what your mission tells you to do. Things will turn out fine. Don't despair; trust the flow of the cosmic cycles. They will naturally help you clean up this mess.

210 degrees: As the test of integrity comes to a close, the danger of losing identity increases, but holding on to the mission is what offers protection, as well as awareness of what has been learned so far.

Stick to your values of integrity, even though you might have to give up some things that no longer match your newfound completeness. As disappointing as it is, you must let them go and accept it. New and better things will come your way. Just know that if you were to keep them in your life, you would have had to bend yourself backwards to please them and face their ever-increasing requests. Eventually you would have had to give up your newfound balance, your identity; you would be basically selling your personal integrity to suit their unbalanced ways. Having found and retrieved the lunar quality, you would have suffered in such a solar-focused system, even more than you did at the beginning of this journey. It is therefore better to recollect your values and strongly identify yourself with those.

216 degrees (strong lunar influence): A passage is erected over which a crossing into a new life becomes possible.

The fact alone that you so firmly stand your ground against low-integrity systems builds a passageway for the lunar energies to re-enter these places. They are now able to find their way in and start to transform them. Slowly but surely, this process gets going and builds speed. It might still look as though things are in favor of the old unbalanced ways, but be assured, this is not so. Things are changing from the inside out now. Redemption from the shadow forces can start, and it becomes possible for you to accomplish your mission. After all, the prerequisite for a life in balance and completeness, peace, and harmony is set up. The lunar energy returns and is also able to take root in your surroundings, just as it took root in you. And with the return of the lunar energy, your environment also starts to move into alignment with the cosmic cycles. This process will still take a while until it is complete, but the old systems lose more and more of their power.

Fairy tale examples:

- The sister of the twelve wild ducks was still neither speaking nor showing any emotion. Her mother-in-law believed she was a witch, and after each childbirth, she stole the young mother's babies from the crib, threw them into a snake pit, and smeared blood on her face. After the third time, the king sentenced his wife to be burned at the stake. *(The old queen is a woman who profits from the solar-focused system and her status in it. Therefore, she is either unwilling to accept or has no feeling for the lunar energy.)* Just when the pile was ablaze, the sister made signs to lay the twelve shirts she had woven around the pile. Twelve wild ducks came flying and each of them snapped up his shirt and flew off with it. *(The sister's relentless effort made it possible to at least disenchant her brothers and thus achieve her mission. In this moment, the balance between the Sun and Moon is now restored for society.)*

- Upon hearing that Rosa had been saved and married, the stepmother pretended to be friendly and brought Rosa an evil gift. Rosa accepted the woven dress with golden threads *(solar-threads)* but was enchanted immediately. She was turned into a golden goose. At the same time, the linden tree stopped chiming, the nightingale stopped singing, and a great sadness fell over the entire kingdom. *(By accepting the gift with the solar-threads, Rosa loses her ability to execute her duty to society. She would need to bring her gained wisdom into society now. The goose, however, stands for the lunar energy and is a symbol of the goddess; therefore, Rosa can remain a representative of the goddess but cannot act in service of others.)*
- All-kinds-of-Fur cooked a soup for the king and put a golden ring in it. The king never tasted a better soup before, found the ring, and called for her. *(The king recognizes the difference in energy "in the soup"—a cyclical energy—and is not afraid to meet it.)* He asked her, "Who are you?" *(He is curious, but she does not yet reveal who she is. Slowly but surely, she builds the passage for him to accept her into his life.)*

225 degrees: It is time to firmly anchor the new reality, otherwise the lunar energy vanishes into oblivion again.

By applying the gained wisdom with great clarity and intent, you leave little room for shadow forces, even though it is not quite over yet.

However, knowing that you are in service of something larger than you, which will bring balance to all, helps you focus on what needs to be done. Be proud of how far you have come, and do not be sad if the acknowledgment you have wanted for so long is not yet given. It is not time for it. But you can work with the lunar energies and rejoice in their creative expression.

230 degrees: A crossroads of destiny shows the road to mastery.

A moment of great importance is here. It is one of destiny's crossroads where your fate takes a turn again. Suddenly, you can envision nothing less than mastery. Since the difficult times recently increased your wisdom in understanding the divine workings, it is easier for you to bring forth situations that are for the highest good of everyone. The lunar energies are very familiar to you, and you easily commune with spirit. All in all, you have great tools and stand in a good position for future success. Now it is up to you to decide exactly how you want to use them. Do you want to learn as much as possible about life's mysteries and teach others? Do you want to heal or advise others? Or use it to give children a loving home or create a beautiful garden? Whatever it is, you are on your road to mastery.

240 degrees: The vision of mastery inspires a new future.

Your experience can now become a living philosophy. You are filled with a vision of what is possible, and you see how things are interconnected. A promise of a better future is tangible, and you even know how it can be achieved. The only dangers are that you remain inactive, passively dreaming of a better world, or in the worst case, that you take on a martyr role. In that case your visions would quickly dissolve into mere daydreams and you'd lose your balance again. So, you must always keep up your values of integrity and individual responsibility and act accordingly.

Fairy tale examples:

- He walked until he got hungry and had no food left. Then he saw a raven with a broken wing and caught him. Just when he was about to kill and eat it, the raven begged for his life. In return, he promised to help him in need. So, the boy let him go and caught a rabbit with a broken leg, who promised the same. The same happened with a fox, so that in the end he said to himself, "Oh well, then I won't eat anything anymore." *(Instead of eating immediately, he decides to collect the favors from magical helpers, which will help him save the princess from the dragon.)*
- The old queen saw her suspicion proven when the twelve wild ducks snatched up the shirts: her daughter-in-law was a witch. But the king ordered his guards not to light the fire yet, so he could watch what happens. *(He recognized his wife's lunar qualities and came to the crossroads of burning his wife or aiming at mastery together with her.)* Then the twelve princes came riding along, as handsome well-grown lads as you'd wish to see. *(The vision of a new future appears in the form of the unenchanted princes. The awareness of the natural Sun and Moon ratio is restored, there are now again twelve solar "brothers" and their lunar "sister" considered in a seasonal turnover.)*

- A white virgin came out of the little house in the woods with the sign, "Here, everyone lives for free." She invited the girl without hands in and said, "Welcome, Her Majesty the Queen." *(The girl without hands is recognized by the goddess in white for what she is: a queen. This anchors her soul's higher purpose to be in a leading position, a hint at the potential of wise leadership.)* The white lady took the baby off her back and held him so that he could drink from his mother's breast. *(Here, the girl lives for free, there are no strings attached. She is safe and can think for the first time about becoming a master and passing on what she has learned to the next generation.)*

245 degrees: What might seem bad at first presents itself as a chance to turn matters around.

A chance is presented to you to turn matters around. You receive the help you need to help yourself.

252 degrees (strong lunar influence): The connection to the lunar energy has become very strong so that wounds can heal.

What you learned during this journey and the strong connection to the lunar energy that you have established now heal your wounds from earlier confrontations with the shadow forces. A kind of second elixir is given to you, tending to your pain. It makes up for all the bad things that happened to you along the way. This new elixir can now help you to consciously transform that which needs to be transformed in your personal life, as well as in society. You can finally understand and witness your work's powerful impact on your own life and that of others.

Consequently, your soul's higher purpose becomes comprehensible at last.

255 degrees: An opportunity like a diamond in the rough presents itself.

A new and better future is starting to take shape for you. It is not quite all as it should be yet, but it is possible that your life wants to take you to an even more interesting place, to before-unthought-of heights. You might want to check out a new option that can be seen on the horizon of your life.

Fairy tale examples:

- The fishermen used a net to catch the golden goose who approached them at night out on the sea, just as the king had ordered. But the goose wildly flapped her wings and called out, "Let me go or hold on tight!" *(Rosa can only come back into the tangible reality if she finds strong support there.)* Suddenly, she changed into snakes, dragons, and other terrible monsters. *(These are other names of the goddess but in her rebirthing aspect. Rosa is therefore between life and death, between this world and the other.)*
- "What's all this about?" asked the princes who were wild ducks before. "My queen is to be burned," said the king, "because she's a witch and because she has eaten up her own babes." *(It all looks very dire for the king and his queen; however, the princes, who are disenchanted now, can help.)* "She hasn't eaten them at all," said the princes. Then the sister

spoke for the first time and told the whole story. The princes took the king and showed him the snake pit where three babes lay playing with adders and toads. *(The young queen's wounds are healed as her babies are found alive and well. The image of the babies playing with snakes and toads implies that they were with the goddess in her re-birthing aspect.)*

- The poor woman asked, "How did you know that I once was a queen?" The white lady said, "I am an angel and God sent me to take care of your child." *(There is a Christian overlay on this tale, making an angel out of the goddess.)* The woman stayed in the house for seven years and was well taken care of. *(She gets a chance to recover from the hardships she had to endure beforehand. Deep healing can happen in this place of divine care.)*

The Sixth Segment of the Cycle

257.08 degrees to 308.34 degrees

Creating a New Future

A new future can be woven by tapping into the full range of cosmic energies.

As the heroine unwaveringly follows her mission, the shadow forces lose their grip on her. This triggers recovery and the necessary change of perspective to become a master. It will mark the end of how things were before. The recovered completeness eventually will bring healthy renewal for all.

By applying what she has learned, the heroine lays a new foundation for her higher purpose to unfold now. She begins to understand the core of the matter. She is in constant communication with spirit, which makes it easier for her to turn ideas into solid matter and to become a master. Therefore, actively dealing with the entire spectrum of creative energies allows for her gained wisdom to begin doing its magic, not only for her own purposes, but also in favor of others. By consciously weaving both the lunar and the solar thread into the cloth of reality, the heroine aims at the highest expression of life. Her high ideals can become a living reality for all, and new visions already start to inspire a future cycle.

The Aspects of the Sixth Segment

257.08 degrees: A change of perspective occurs. It is the end of what was before.

Deep recovery takes place, which also transforms your viewpoint. You may have a feeling of having arrived at last. You may want to make some fundamental external changes in your life, which will mirror those that recently occurred on the inside. Since your actions were intuitively attuned to the cosmic order, new and exciting opportunities open for you. You need to solidly ground yourself in the physical. This prepares a good base for future mastery.

270 degrees: Life is experienced from the changed viewpoint, which marks a new beginning.

Your life takes a turn as things are revealed. A new and wholesome order establishes itself. You are redeemed from past issues, and your serious hopes and dreams manifest. Residues from old wounds are cleaned away. Things you have been working on for a long time come to a new level and start to make sense from a higher viewpoint.

280 degrees: The foundation for a new life is laid.

You are appreciated and rewarded for your qualities and past actions. However, not all things are how you want them to be yet. You feel pulled to continue to weave your future with the right activities and translate what you learned into reality. You are on the verge of becoming a master. The cloth of reality you now weave corresponds to the level of integrity you tested a few years earlier. You no longer tolerate lies or falsehoods. Your soul's higher purpose is empowered. Dealing actively with the entire spectrum of the creative qualities facilitates completeness.

Fairy tale examples:

- Wassilissa dug a deep hole in the ground and buried the skull, which had burned her stepmother and step-sisters. *(A change of perspective is needed; she may no longer rely on the magic attributes of the skull.)* Then she went to live with an old woman and did not like sitting idle. *(A new era begins.)* "Buy me some flax, the best and finest to be found anywhere, and at least I can spin." (*It is time to get active and spin a new future. A young girl wants a partner and not to live alone with an old woman.)*
- God's grace lets the girl's cut-off hands grow back, and she remained in the care of the angel. *(The girl gets to experience a kind of benign care, which heals all her wounds from a violent life.)* The king came home from the battlefield, but he found his wife and son were gone. *(The change of perspective is directly in the story. It now focuses on the king.)* He found out that they were almost assassinated and were sent away for their own protection. *(Wrongdoings are revealed, and he is given the opportunity for a new start under better circumstances.)*
- The king had his babies taken out of the snake pit at once, and the old queen's deeds came to light. *(Recovery takes place*

and wrongdoings are exposed.) The evil queen spoke her own doom and was punished.

285 degrees: The divine creative energies can be tapped into to create a new life.

All the divine creation energies are available to you. If you keep to the cosmic laws, they can be tapped into.

288 degrees: A legacy is created.

You feel empowered to affect something that will leave a mark beyond the current moment, even beyond your life, be it in your family, your surroundings, or your society. Wouldn't you want to use your skills to make this world a better place? The necessary tools are at your disposal. Now you can shine the light you always wanted to and leave a legacy.

300 degrees: What once was only a vision can now become a living reality.

By now, you easily transform ideals into real life, using your sense of integrity and cosmic alignment as a guideline. The support you receive opens new visions for your next heroic cycle, which will soon begin.

305 degrees (strong lunar influence): The power of the alignment keeps inspiring you.

You are solidly connected with the spiritual realm. There is vivid communication, and you can consult your guides any time. They promote your soul's higher purpose, which makes it possible to grow way beyond your limits and reach things you felt were out of reach for you.

Fairy tale examples:

- But the king took his wife, their three children, and the twelve princes. They all went home to their father and mother. *(All of the divine creation energies are available now and hold the vision of a new and healthy renewal of the society.)*
- The old woman brought flax for Wassilissa, who spun so well that the thread came out as even and fine as a hair but could not be woven. Then Wassilissa got her little doll, set food and drink before it, and asked its help. *(Working with the divine creation energies asks for constant communication between spirit and human.)* The doll came alive and said, "Bring me an old frame and an old basket and some hairs from a horse's mane, and I will arrange everything for thee." *(Spirit helps to easily transform ideas into matter and promotes the human's higher purpose.)*
- All-kinds-of-Fur put on her dress that shimmered like the stars and entered the hall. The king had never seen such a beautiful princess and danced with her. As they were dancing, without her noticing it, he put her golden ring on her finger. *(The dancing and the ring are a symbol of the entire spectrum of creative energies and their cyclical turning.)* As it ended, she ran away and disappeared. But because she had stayed for too long, she was not able to take off her star dress

anymore. She threw the furs over it, made her face and hands dirty again, and hid in her little stable. In her haste, she left one finger clean. *(She can no longer remain invisible; the world wants to see the light she shines. The visions for a new future arise, and spirit, which does not let her take off the star dress, promotes her soul's higher purpose: to be the princess she is.)*

The Seventh Segment of the Cycle

308.34 degrees to 360 degrees

Reaching Mastery

Wise leadership is established and there is harvest and celebration. The formerly missing lunar energy has been restored to personal life and into society.

The frame for mastery is set up. The heroine only needs to act in attunement with Spirit and the cycles. Being in tune with the cosmic order brings out her wise leadership and lets her become a master. Destiny presents its harvest to her. What was initially missing is finally present. Resistance, adversaries, and shadow forces have long lost their power. Peace and happiness can be reaped.

The old ways are completely transformed. What initially had been only a hope and a vision has turned into a solid reality. Every aspect of life is empowered, bringing on peace, love, and abundance. At the same time, the happy ending carries the promise of a new cycle, where mastery will serve to refine balance in other areas of life.

The Aspects of the Seventh Segment

308.34 degrees: Mastery is reached.

By relying on your alignment to the cosmic order and acting accordingly, you are developing the qualities of a master. Then, you also recognize mastery all around you. It comes with the responsibility to meet and greet your environment with respect and reverence, be they humans or creatures from another realm. Your soul rejoices because she is finally getting to live the bliss of her higher purpose. As much as your higher purpose is in service of others, it is also a blessing for your own soul.

315 degrees: Wise leadership exists at the highest level.

You are leading at the highest level and can trust that the environment you live in also corresponds to that level. During your long journey, you have started to weave a web of life for yourself and for your environment that is aligned to the divine laws. It is a web of dreams. It creates peace, happiness, and abundance and heals what needs to be healed. Your soul knows you have reached mastery.

320 degrees: Time of harvest and letting go of the work.

The decision at the earlier crossroads of destiny presents its harvest. Tangible results are finally showing.

Fairy tale examples:

- The princess from the castle on the pillar in the ocean came on to the boat and chose the nicest of cloths *(she recognized a masterfully woven piece)*, but she did not notice that the seer was rowing the boat away from the shore. *(The seer corresponds to her own mastery and has peace, happiness, and abundance in mind.)* He brought her to the little sorcerer, who kept the sun-horse captive. She agreed to help the seer free the horse. *(For the seer, the work will finally come to an end.)*

- The king was in search of his wife for seven long years. He neither ate nor drank; it was only God that sustained him. *(He walks through life like a master now, letting go of being a king. This creates peace in him and will make it possible for him to find his wife.)* Finally, he came to the house where the angel took care of his wife and him. He took a rest and covered his face with a fabric *(this is their newly woven destiny and shows his mastery)* and he fell asleep. "Your husband has come," said the angel. *(This is the moment of harvest.)*
- The prince heeded the old woman's advice *(wise leadership)* to dress his wife, the golden goose, in the same shirt that originally put the spell on her. Rosa changed back into her human shape. At the same time, the linden tree began to chime, the nightingale began to sing, and all was pure bliss and joy. *(Mastery is recognized all around them. It is the moment of reaping happiness.)*

324 degrees: A new and different future is triggered.

The outcome of this cycle already inspires your next cycle. It is a solid foundation for a new future and already holds new potentials. Where do you feel drawn to next?

330 degrees: What was initially missing is now fully present.

If you take stock and look back on your heroic journey, you see that what was missing in the beginning of the cycle is now integrated in your daily life. Do you remember which expression of the lunar energy was originally missing from your life at 30 degrees?

334.38 degrees (strong lunar influence): Everything falls into the right place, just as it should be.

You have come a long way and can be proud of yourself. Celebrate and enjoy. Your life now holds the promise of renewal and future success, as the lunar energy is well-rooted in your awareness. You look forward to a bright future and already envision new tasks. Now, you might find new spirit guides and/or further deepen your connection to the spirit realm.

342 degrees: Stepping back through destiny's gate.

As you step back through what feels like a gateway, you find your old life so transformed that it is hard to remember how it once used to be. Everything has changed so much for the better since you first stepped through destiny's gate at 18 degrees in search of the missing lunar energy. You are now enriched, calm, and centered. The initial hopes have become a reality, and best of all, you know how to bring about solutions at any time. At the beginning you trespassed the gate of destiny to find solutions; now you are crossing back with a toolset of mastery that creates solutions. It is know-how that cannot be taken from you.

347.14 degrees: All divine creative energies are honored.

As you tend to your communication with spirit and consciously uphold your alignment with the cosmic order, you start to consider which other areas of your life call to be balanced.

354 degrees: The new is already calling.

As the original vision at the beginning of this cycle has become a manifested reality in your everyday life, you hear an inner calling to tackle another big project that needs refinement and balance. Which other expression of the lunar energy calls to be expressed? To what new level could you take your soul's higher purpose?

360 degrees: At the same time, the end of the cycle is the call for a new hero's journey.

The achieved balance and gained wisdom want to be applied in all areas of life. Soon the question will arise: Is there a place in your life where consciousness could be raised further? This is where your attention will go next. You will begin to perceive it as an imbalance, even though it is not as severe as the imbalance you noticed at the beginning of your last journey. However, you do feel enticed to refine your awareness further and thus continue the adventure called life.

Fairy tale examples:

- The bride's servant, who was the real princess, was sent for. *(The real princess, the lunar energy went missing during the war.)* The king recognized his rightful bride, who told him everything that happened to her. The couple was led to their wedding chamber and the crowd began to sing an old wedding song. *(The seeds of truth are planted, and they all look forward to a happy future of healthy renewal.)*

- The fabric fell off his face and the king saw his wife and son for the first time in seven years. They were now happily reunited. *(He displays a fatherly love, which she never had experienced, since her father cut her off her hands. In this happy ending, too, lies the promise of two masters, who have found each other and will create a balanced future.)*
- The seer found the little sorcerer's power hidden inside a golden egg *(the little sorcerer held the lunar energy captive)*. The seer drank it and took it over. *(He is now the carrier of the lunar power.)* Then, he took the sun-horse *(the solar power)* and rode back through the seven lands until he crossed the border to the land of darkness again *(crossing back through the initial gate of destiny)*. As soon as he got there, his sun-horse made everything bright, the flowers began to bloom, and the hearts of the people rejoiced. *(The Sun and Moon cycles are restored. This land that was initially all dark will now prosper thanks to the rhythms of day and night and the seasons.)*

Appendix A

Where are You Located on Your Journey?

Please note that the indication of your age in the tables is generalized. It uses the Neolithic Aubrey Circle at Stonehenge as a model. Since the lunar nodes move three degrees per day, the fifty-six Aubrey holes look like they were placed so that every four months the progress of the lunar nodes could be marked on a pillar. Tracking the lunar nodes like this represents their average speed around the zodiac. However, your age might be slightly off by a few days or even a month when you calculate the distance from the transiting north node to your personal north node placement. Therefore, do not take the ages indicated here as set in stone, pun intended; the stones that were set to represent them obviously must have been for general use. Therefore, you must allow for a certain amount of flexibility.

Where you see empty spaces in the tables, there seems to be an astrological aspect missing, and I was not able to identify the meaning of its degree. If you can detect it, please share your insights with me; I'd be delighted to compare notes (andrea@andreahofman.com).

First Hero's Journey/Developmental Cycle

From birth to 18 years and 7 months of age

Your Age year/month		Aspect Degrees
Birth	First Segment	0 degrees
00.04		6 degrees
00.08		12.86 degrees
01.00		18 degrees
01.04		25.71 degrees
01.08		30 degrees
02.00		36 degrees / 40 degrees
02.03		45 degrees
02.07	Second Segment	51.42 degrees
02.11		55 degrees
03.03		60 degrees
03.07		72 degrees
03.11		75 degrees
04.03		80 degrees
04.07		90 degrees
04.11		
05.03	Third Segment	102.85 degrees
05.07		108 degrees
05.11		115 degrees
06.03		120 degrees
06.07		130 degrees
06.11		135 degrees
07.03		144 degrees
07.07		150 degrees
07.11	Fourth Segment	154.28 degrees
08.03		160 degrees

08.07		165 degrees
08.11		
09.03		180 degrees
09.07		
09.11		195 degrees
10.03		200 degrees
10.07	Fifth Segment	205.42 degrees
10.11		210 degrees
11.03		216 degrees
11.07		225 degrees
11.11		230 degrees
12.03		240 degrees
12.07		245 degrees
12.11		252 degrees
13.03	Sixth Segment	257.08 degrees
13.07		
13.11		270 degrees
14.03		280 degrees
14.07		285 degrees
14.11		288 degrees
15.03		300 degrees
15.07		305 degrees
15.11	Seventh Segment	308.34 degrees
16.03		315 degrees
16.07		324 degrees / 320 degrees
16.11		330 degrees
17.03		334.38 degrees
17.07		342 degrees
17.11		347.14 degrees
18.03		354 degrees

Second Hero's Journey/Developmental Cycle

from 18 years and 7 months to 37 years and 3 months of age

Your Age year/month		Aspect Degrees
18.07	First Segment	0 degrees
18.11		6 degrees
19.03		12.86 degrees
19.07		18 degrees
19.11		25.71 degrees
20.03		30 degrees
20.07		36 degrees / 40 degrees
20.11		45 degrees
21.03	Second Segment	51.42 degrees
21.07		55 degrees
21.11		60 degrees
22.03		72 degrees
22.07		75 degrees
22.11		80 degrees
23.03		90 degrees
23.07		
23.11	Third Segment	102.85 degrees
24.03		108 degrees
24.07		115 degrees
24.11		120 degrees
25.03		130 degrees
25.07		135 degrees
25.11		144 degrees
26.03		150 degrees
26.07	Fourth Segment	154.28 degrees
26.11		160 degrees

27.03		165 degrees
27.07		
27.11		180 degrees
28.03		
28.07		195 degrees
28.11		200 degrees
29.03	Fifth Segment	205.42 degrees
29.07		210 degrees
29.11		216 degrees
30.03		225 degrees
30.07		230 degrees
30.11		240 degrees
31.03		245 degrees
31.07		252 degrees
31.11	Sixth Segment	257.08 degrees
32.03		
32.07		270 degrees
32.11		280 degrees
33.03		285 degrees
33.07		288 degrees
33.11		300 degrees
34.03		305 degrees
34.07	Seventh Segment	308.34 degrees
34.11		315 degrees
35.03		324 degrees / 320 degrees
35.07		330 degrees
35.11		334.38 degrees
36.03		342 degrees
36.07		347.14 degrees
36.11		354 degrees

Third Hero's Journey/Developmental Cycle

from 37 years and 3 months to 55 years and 11 months of age

Your Age year/month		Aspect Degrees
37.03	First Segment	0 degrees
37.07		6 degrees
37.11		12.86 degrees
38.03		18 degrees
38.07		25.71 degrees
38.11		30 degrees
39.03		36 degrees / 40 degrees
39.07		45 degrees
39.11	Second Segment	51.42 degrees
40.03		55 degrees
40.07		60 degrees
40.11		72 degrees
41.03		75 degrees
41.07		80 degrees
41.11		90 degrees
42.03		
42.07	Third Segment	102.85 degrees
42.11		108 degrees
43.03		115 degrees
43.07		120 degrees
43.11		130 degrees
44.03		135 degrees
44.07		144 degrees
44.11		150 degrees
45.03	Fourth Segment	154.28 degrees
45.07		160 degrees

45.11		165 degrees
46.03		
46.07		180 degrees
46.11		
47.03		195 degrees
47.07		200 degrees
47.11	Fifth Segment	205.42 degrees
48.03		210 degrees
48.07		216 degrees
48.11		225 degrees
49.03		230 degrees
49.07		240 degrees
49.11		245 degrees
50.03		252 degrees
50.07	Sixth Segment	257.08 degrees
50.11		
51.03		270 degrees
51.07		280 degrees
51.11		285 degrees
52.03		288 degrees
52.07		300 degrees
52.11		305 degrees
53.03	Seventh Segment	308.34 degrees
53.07		315 degrees
53.11		324 degrees / 320 degrees
54.03		330 degrees
54.07		334.38 degrees
54.11		342 degrees
55.03		347.14 degrees
55.07		354 degrees

Fourth Hero's Journey/Developmental Cycle

from 55 years and 11 months to 74 years and 6 months of age

Your Age year/month		Aspect Degrees
55.11	First Segment	0 degrees
56.02		6 degrees
56.06		12.86 degrees
56.10		18 degrees
57.02		25.71 degrees
57.06		30 degrees
57.10		36 degrees / 40 degrees
58.02		45 degrees
58.06	Second Segment	51.42 degrees
58.10		55 degrees
59.02		60 degrees
59.06		72 degrees
59.10		75 degrees
60.02		80 degrees
60.06		90 degrees
60.10		
61.02	Third Segment	102.85 degrees
61.06		108 degrees
61.10		115 degrees
62.02		120 degrees
62.06		130 degrees
62.10		135 degrees
63.02		144 degrees
63.06		150 degrees
63.10	Fourth Segment	154.28 degrees
64.02		160 degrees

64.06		165 degrees
64.10		
65.02		180 degrees
65.06		
65.10		195 degrees
66.02		200 degrees
66.06	Fifth Segment	205.42 degrees
66.10		210 degrees
67.02		216 degrees
67.06		225 degrees
67.10		230 degrees
68.02		240 degrees
68.06		245 degrees
68.10		252 degrees
69.02	Sixth Segment	257.08 degrees
69.06		
69.10		270 degrees
70.02		280 degrees
70.06		285 degrees
70.10		288 degrees
71.02		300 degrees
71.06		305 degrees
71.10	Seventh Segment	308.34 degrees
72.02		315 degrees
72.06		324 degrees / 320 degrees
72.10		330 degrees
73.02		334.38 degrees
73.06		342 degrees
73.10		347.14 degrees
74.02		354 degrees

Fifth Hero's Journey/Developmental Cycle

from 74 years and 6 months to 93 years and 1 month of age

Your Age year/month		Aspect Degrees
74.06	First Segment	0 degrees
74.09		6 degrees
75.01		12.86 degrees
75.05		18 degrees
75.09		25.71 degrees
76.01		30 degrees
76.05		36 degrees / 40 degrees
76.09		45 degrees
77.01	Second Segment	51.42 degrees
77.05		55 degrees
77.09		60 degrees
78.01		72 degrees
78.05		75 degrees
78.09		80 degrees
79.01		90 degrees
79.05		
79.09	Third Segment	102.85 degrees
80.01		108 degrees
80.05		115 degrees
80.09		120 degrees
81.01		130 degrees
81.05		135 degrees
81.09		144 degrees
82.01		150 degrees
82.05	Fourth Segment	154.28 degrees
82.09		160 degrees

83.01		165 degrees
83.05		
83.09		180 degrees
84.01		
84.05		195 degrees
84.09		200 degrees
85.01	Fifth Segment	205.42 degrees
85.05		210 degrees
85.09		216 degrees
86.01		225 degrees
86.05		230 degrees
86.09		240 degrees
87.01		245 degrees
87.05		252 degrees
87.09	Sixth Segment	257.08 degrees
88.01		
88.05		270 degrees
88.09		280 degrees
89.01		285 degrees
89.05		288 degrees
89.09		300 degrees
90.01		305 degrees
90.05	Seventh Segment	308.34 degrees
90.09		315 degrees
91.01		324 degrees / 320 degrees
91.05		330 degrees
91.09		334.38 degrees
92.01		342 degrees
92.05		347.14 degrees
92.09		354 degrees

Sixth Hero's Journey/Developmental Cycle

from 93 years and 1 month to 111 years and 9 months old

Your Age year/month		Aspect Degrees
93.01	First Segment	0 degrees
93.05		6 degrees
93.09		12.86 degrees
94.01		18 degrees
94.05		25.71 degrees
94.09		30 degrees
95.01		36 degrees / 40 degrees
95.05		45 degrees
95.09	Second Segment	51.42 degrees
96.01		55 degrees
96.05		60 degrees
96.09		72 degrees
97.01		75 degrees
97.05		80 degrees
97.09		90 degrees
98.01		
98.05	Third Segment	102.85 degrees
98.09		108 degrees
99.01		115 degrees
99.05		120 degrees
99.09		130 degrees
100.01		135 degrees
100.05		144 degrees
100.09		150 degrees
101.01	Fourth Segment	154.28 degrees
101.05		160 degrees

101.09		165 degrees
102.01		
102.05		180 degrees
102.09		
103.01		195 degrees
103.05		200 degrees
103.09	Fifth Segment	205.42 degrees
104.01		210 degrees
104.05		216 degrees
104.09		225 degrees
105.01		230 degrees
105.05		240 degrees
105.09		245 degrees
106.01		252 degrees
106.05	Sixth Segment	257.08 degrees
106.09		
107.01		270 degrees
107.05		280 degrees
107.09		285 degrees
108.01		288 degrees
108.05		300 degrees
108.09		305 degrees
109.01	Seventh Segment	308.34 degrees
109.05		315 degrees
109.09		324 degrees / 320 degrees
110.01		330 degrees
110.05		334.38 degrees
110.09		342 degrees
111.01		347.14 degrees
111.05		354 degrees

Appendix B

Beauty and the Beast with Aspect Key Sentences

The tale "Beauty and the Beast" was collected in France, where it had been told in the countryside by the illiterate folk. Jeanne-Marie Leprince de Beaumont put it in a polished written form and adapted the style to suit the seventeenth century French court. At the time, it was very popular to add a moral at the end of each fairy tale, which seemed to amuse the French nobility. The story therefore, on first sight, seems to talk of a young girl who must marry a beast of a man—dominant, grumpy, and ugly. If the poor girl is only virtuous enough, a good fairy godmother will have mercy and turn the beast into a beautiful prince.

However, as usual, there is more underneath the obvious interpretation of the zeitgeist. Despite its embellished style, the tale still follows the Neolithic aspect circle. The aforementioned study found the tale to be as old as 4,000 years. The tale's origin thus might coincide with the time when, at the site of Stonehenge, the Aubrey calendar was replaced and a new use for the bluestones was found. It therefore must have been ever more important to keep telling calendrical stories according to the old balanced calendar, to remind people of the cosmic order and not suppress the lunar energies. And if they were already suppressed in a society, then it would instruct people how to retrieve it. The tale obviously wants to remind humans how to get back into contact with the divine, even if the goddess appears in her scary and ugly aspect, even if she is more like a beast than a lovely fairy.

Looking at the aspect build-up once again reveals the hidden message of the tale. When stripping it off its seventeenth-century veneer, a vivid painting of a matriarchal, prehistoric worldview emerges, just as we have seen in Part I of this book. It soon becomes evident that the Beast is the demonized mother goddess. As in other tales, we find in this story the information on how a young girl can remember her divine origin and start to move herself and her surroundings back into alignment with the natural cosmic order. By following the instruction of the tale, therefore any young girl, no matter what epoch she lives in, can do the same.

To cut to the core, I allowed myself to leave out some of the stylistically enriched passages. However, as usual, I neither altered the sequence of the storyline nor any of the sentences.[64]

64 See entire tale on wiki common source en.wikisource.org/wiki/Old_time_stories_(Perrault,_Robinson)/Beauty_and_the_Beast or on pitt.edu/~dash/beauty.html

The First Segment: Discovering that something is missing

Zero degrees (strong lunar influence): Life is incomplete, a notion that triggers an in-limbo state, resulting in feelings of isolation and separation.	
ONCE upon a time there lived a merchant who was exceedingly rich. He had six children—three boys and three girls—and being a sensible man he spared no expense upon their education... All his daughters were pretty, but the youngest especially was admired by everybody.... The two elder girls were very arrogant as a result of their wealth;... The two eldest said they would never marry unless they could find a duke, or at least a count. But Beauty . . . very politely thanked all who proposed marriage to her, and said that she was too young at present, and that she wished to keep her father company for several years yet. Suddenly, the merchant lost his fortune, the sole property which remained to him being a small house in the country, a long way from the capital. With tears he broke it to his children that they would have to move to this house, whereby working like peasants they might just be able to live...	*In the introduction of the story, an imbalance of values in this family shows: Two girls think but of getting themselves a rich husband. Beauty, however, wants to live by values of the heart. The imbalance becomes noticeable when the father loses his fortune and with it his status in society. Suddenly, they no longer belong to the nobility and are reduced to being peasants.*

6 degrees: A vision of a complete reality is harbored.	
There were even several worthy men who would have married her, despite the fact that she was now penniless; but she told them she could not make up her mind to leave her poor father in his misfortune,	*Beauty lets herself be guided by the heart and prefers the simple life, close to nature and close to her father.*

12.86 degrees (strong lunar influence): New opportunities come up. They offer to make this vision a reality.	
and that she intended to go with him to the country, to comfort him and help him to work.	*She seems to already envision a better life in the country side. She understands that it is spirit offering them nourishment directly from the soil.*

18 degrees: Destiny's gate stands wide open and calls the human to go change what desperately needs to be changed. The hope for a quick fix is enticing.	
When they were established in the country the merchant and his family started working on the land. Beauty used to rise at four o'clock in the morning, and was busy all day looking after the house, and preparing dinner for the family. At first she found it very hard, for she was not accustomed to work like a servant, but at the end of a couple of months she grew stronger, and her health was improved by the work.	*Destiny offers them to walk through an open gate into a new kind of life. The family survives thanks to working the land. The rhythm and work aligned with that of nature brings Beauty back to an inner balance and makes her stronger.*

25.71 degrees: A glance at the missing quality is given. What may have been dormant due to social conditionings is being re-awoken.	
When she had leisure she read, or played the harpsichord, or sang at her spinning wheel.	*Reading poetry and making music elevates Beauty's mind and lets her have an inner communication with spirit. When working at the spinning wheel, she is attuning herself to the spinning movement of the cosmos. Therefore, she is consciously starting to work with the divine creative forces to spin herself a new future.*

<table>
<tr><th colspan="2">30 degrees: With the recognition of completeness also comes the sudden awareness of what has been missing all along.</th></tr>
<tr><td>Her two sisters, on the other hand, were bored to death; they did not get up till ten o'clock in the morning, and they idled about all day. Their only diversion was to bemoan the beautiful clothes they used to wear and the company they used to keep.</td><td>Like in Mother Holle, the negative example of the two sisters clarifies the point of the tale. These girls lack the sense of rhythm (of the changing day and night lights, the Sun and the Moon) and only focus on themselves and their own needs.</td></tr>
</table>

<table>
<tr><th colspan="2">36 degrees: A surge of optimism and a feeling of omnipotence entice the human to move on.</th></tr>
<tr><td>The good merchant did not share the opinion of his two daughters, for he knew that Beauty was more fitted to shine in company than her sisters.</td><td>The father, however, recognizes the qualities inherent in Beauty.</td></tr>
</table>

<table>
<tr><th colspan="2">40 degrees: Mostly unnoticed, the potential for completeness is growing.</th></tr>
<tr><td>He was greatly impressed by the girl's good qualities, and especially by her patience...
They had been living for a year in this seclusion when the merchant received a letter informing him that a ship on which he had some merchandise had just come safely home. The news nearly turned the heads of the two elder girls... When they saw their father ready to set out they begged him to bring them back dresses, furs, caps, and finery of every kind. Beauty asked for nothing,... (but) 'please bring me a rose, for there are none here.'...</td><td>With patience, Beauty surrenders to the ups and downs of life, which are the cycles of the luminaries. Mostly unnoticed, she is growing toward a more balanced life. She asks for a rose, which, like the lotus flower in Asia, is the symbol of the highest consciousness and wholeness in European cultures. It stands for reaching completeness of the self. This is the new potential that is growing.</td></tr>
</table>

45 degrees: The hope for a new future triggers the impulse to move on, but at the same time, old patterns are pulling back.	
The merchant duly set forth; but when he reached his destination there was a law-suit over his merchandise, and after much trouble he returned poorer than he had been before.	*The old ways no longer work, even though the merchant might want to return to his old life. Things must change profoundly, and balance must be restored, before a new kind of wealth and happiness can be established.*

The Second Segment: Getting to Know the Missing Energy

51.42 degrees: Support is given to advance matters. Depending on the degree of incompleteness, the missing quality can be perceived for what it truly is, or it is mistaken for something dangerous, evil or ugly.	
With only thirty miles to go before reaching home, he was already looking forward to the pleasure of seeing his children again, when he found he had to pass through a large wood. Here he lost himself. It was snowing horribly; the wind was so strong that twice he was thrown from his horse, and when night came on he made up his mind he must either die of hunger and cold or be eaten by the wolves that he could hear howling all about him. Suddenly he saw, at the end of a long avenue of trees, a strong light. It seemed to be some distance away, but he walked towards it, and presently discovered that it came from a large palace, which was all lit up. The merchant thanked heaven for sending him this help, and hastened to the castle.	*As if a secret force were pulling the strings of destiny, the father is getting lost in a large wood. It is a dire situation, as in many other tales in this place. Suddenly, the father no longer is protected by wealth and luxury, but finds himself exposed to the wildness of life. He is in direct contact with nature and suddenly realizes that this situation is physically about life and death. In this very moment, spirit intervenes.*

55 degrees (strong lunar influence): Becoming equipped to recover the missing quality.	
To his surprise, however, he found no one about in the courtyards.... He entered a large room; here there was a good fire, and a table laden with food, but with a place laid for one only. ...Being no longer able to resist his hunger he took a chicken and devoured it in two mouthfuls, trembling.	*Beauty's father is sustained, and his life saved. Even though he doesn't notice it yet, it is the goddess who supports him. She guides him to recover the missing lunar quality in his life. It will let him eventually open his eyes beyond the needs for possession.*

60 degrees: Getting to know the surroundings. Something potentially life changing is beginning to take shape.	
Then he drank several glasses of wine, and becoming bolder ventured out of the room. He went through several magnificently furnished apartments, and finally found a room with a very good bed. It was now past midnight, and as he was very tired he decided to shut the door and go to bed.	*After his foremost physical needs are met, he can start to get familiar with this mysterious place and the workings of the divine. Being all alone in a strange place, he gets to explore things with new and open eyes.*

72 degrees: New and creative ways of interacting with the surroundings.	
It was ten o'clock the next morning when he rose, and he was greatly astonished to find a new suit in place of his own, which had been spoilt. 'This palace,' he said to himself, 'must surely belong to some good fairy, who has taken pity on my plight.'	*By putting on the new suit, he reacts to what the goddess laid out for him. He recognizes her as "a good fairy" and begins to interact with her.*

75 degrees: Careful discernment is required.	
He looked out of the window. The snow had vanished, and his eyes rested instead upon arbours of flowers a charming spectacle. He went back to the room where he had supped the night before, and found there a little table with a cup of chocolate on it. 'I thank you, Madam Fairy,' he said aloud, ' for being so kind as to think of my breakfast.'	*Where there was snow, there is now summer. Now, he is discerning the situation. Where is he? Whose place is this? The scenery reminds us of Mother Holle's world, where flowers bloom on green meadows. He does acknowledge its beauty and discerns it as the workings of a fairy.*

80 degrees (strong lunar influence): A protective sphere is provided to further strengthen the connection to the missing quality.	
Having drunk his chocolate the good man went forth to look for his horse. As he passed under a bower of roses he remembered that Beauty had asked for one, and he plucked a spray from a mass of blooms. The very same moment he heard a terrible noise, and saw a beast coming towards him which was so hideous that he came near to fainting.	*Here, the roses grow that his daughter wished for. In this time of year (it is still wintertime) roses only bloom in the otherworldly garden of the goddess. Beauty must have known this. So, plucking one signals her father's (unconscious) intention to contribute to Beauty's higher consciousness and to help her reach completeness of the self. With the action of plucking the flowers, he agrees to collaborate with the goddess, nature, and the cosmic cycles. He will be under her protection, even though it does not look like it now. Yet from Mother Holle and Baba Yaga, we know that they are not just nice old ladies or lovely looking fairies. On the contrary, the goddess can look frightening, even appalling, just like the beast that enters the scene here.*

90 degrees: A threshold is crossed. The old must now be left behind.	
'Ungrateful wretch!' said the Beast, in a dreadful voice; 'I have saved your life by receiving you into my castle, and in return for my trouble you steal that which I love better than anything in the world, my roses. You shall pay for this with your life! I give you fifteen minutes to make your peace with Heaven!'	*It is the goddess in her death-aspect. Therefore, she appears like a beast. Well, he cannot come into her realm and just rip-off roses without learning that everything has its season in nature. He came straight out of wintertime, taking roses is therefore like signing a contract. While it holds the promise of a new summer, new beauty and riches, it must also come with a new consciousness. Unless he is willing to learn about the cycles and transform his way of looking at life's abundance, he will be devoured by the beast, the death-aspect of the goddess.*

The Third Segment: Finding the Elixir and a Mission

102.85 degrees: Struggle and isolation make the missing quality painfully evident. Yet it is here where reconnection to the missing can be permanently established.	
The merchant threw himself on his knees and wrung his hands. 'Pardon, my lord!' he cried; 'one of my daughters had asked for a rose, and I did not dream I should be giving offence by picking one.'	*He becomes painfully aware that he has no choice, either he surrenders to the rules of nature and starts to move with them, or he will die.*

105 degrees: Preparation for something unusual to happen.	
'I am not called *my lord,'* answered the monster, 'but *The Beast*. I have no liking for compliments, but prefer people to say what they think. Do not hope therefore to soften me by flattery.'	*Flattery and courtesy do not hold up in the face of the goddess and her cosmic laws. Even though it is not spelled out here, the father is offered to find a more natural way full of virtue, integrity, and higher consciousness. (This could become his and Beauty's higher purpose and seems to have intuitively been aspired by Beauty when asking for a rose). If there were no such option, the beast would have killed him without much words.*

108 degrees: (strong lunar influence): A life-sustaining elixir is found or given. It sets free a before-unknown inner strength, which stems from the growing connection to the formerly missing quality.	
'You have daughters, you say; well, I am willing to pardon you if one of your daughters will come, of her own choice, to die in your place.'	*To re-learn the natural ways, it is best if one of his daughters takes up an apprenticeship with the goddess, like in Mother Holle. Since women are the ones who have a monthly menstrual cycle, have babies, and nurture them, they are better suited to learn to be the representative of the goddess. In any case, with her wish for a rose, Beauty already signaled her willingness. So, the elixir the father receives here is nothing but his own precious life and the chance to make his future (and that of his children) a better one by collaborating with the goddess. This could become his and Beauty's mission, if he accepts the deal.*

115 degrees: New hope is gained, and again, careful discernment is required.	
'Do not argue with me—go! And swear that if your daughters refuse to die in your place you will come back again in three months.' The good man had no intention of sacrificing one of his daughters to this hideous monster, but he thought that at least he might have the pleasure of kissing them once again. He therefore swore to return, and the Beast told him he could go when he wished. 'I do not wish you to go emptyhanded,' he added; 'return to the room where you slept; you will find there a large empty box. Fill it with what you will; I will have it sent home for you.' With these words the Beast withdrew, leaving the merchant to reflect that if he must indeed die, at all events he would have the consolation of providing for his poor children.	*The goddess allows no arguing. She speaks of dying, but it is the dying of the old ways which she refers to. He needs to discern for himself, what is right and helpful in his situation.*

120 degrees: The promise of fulfillment can be felt, which now drives forward.	
He went back to the room where he had slept. He found there a large number of gold pieces, and with these he filled the box the Beast had mentioned.	*The goddess gives him an example of her generosity. It is her promise of a better future, when collaborating with her.*

130 degrees: Arriving at destiny's crossroads. It is a turning point, the result of former efforts.	
Having closed the latter, he took his horse, which was still in the stable, and set forth from the palace, as melancholic now as he had been joyous when he entered it. The horse of its own accord took one of the forest roads, and in a few hours the good man reached his own little house. His children crowded round him, but at sight of them, instead of welcoming their caresses, he burst into tears.	*His horse carries him back. Horses symbolize the Moon and her cyclical rhythm. Therefore, even if the father does not notice it yet, he already is moving with the cycles. His and Beauty's mission to start a collaboration with the goddess/nature has already begun. He is at destiny's crossroads: What is he going to tell his family now that he is safe and sound back in his old life?*

135 degrees: The opportunity to purposefully reshape fate comes with the requirement to think and act differently.	
In his hand was the bunch of roses which he had brought for Beauty, and he gave it to her with these words: 'Take these roses, Beauty; it is dearly that your poor father will have to pay for them.' Thereupon he told his family of the dire adventure which had befallen him. On hearing the tale the two elder girls were in a great commotion, and began to upbraid Beauty for not weeping as they did.... 'It would be quite useless to weep,' said Beauty. 'Why should I lament my father's death? He is not going to die. Since the monster agrees to accept a daughter instead, I intend to offer myself to appease his fury.'... 'No, sister,' said her three brothers; 'you shall not die; we will go in quest of this monster, and will perish under his blows if we cannot kill him.'... Words were useless. Beauty was quite determined to go to this wonderful palace, and her sisters were not sorry, for they regarded her good qualities with deep jealousy.	*It is Beauty who initially provoked the turn of destiny by asking for the rose, so it is she who has the courage to face the intensifying energies. She recognizes the opportunity to purposefully reshape her own fate and that of her family. The fear and her sisters' jealousy are hidden shadows that surface now. They will have to be overcome.*

144 degrees (strong lunar influence): A relapse to the past can and must be avoided now if the right effort is made. Calm inward focus helps to be clearly determined and not fall back into old habits.	
The merchant was so taken up with the sorrow of losing his daughter that he forgot all about the box which he had filled with gold. To his astonishment, when he had shut the door of his room and was about to retire for the night, there it was at the side of his bed! He decided not to tell his children that he had become so rich.... He did confide his secret to Beauty, however....	*The merchant is already so attuned to the divine that boxes full of gold are no longer the first thing on his mind. Still, as he opens the chest, the bridge back from his world to the realm of the goddess is erected and he experiences how rich life could be when attuned to the goddess's horn of plenty. By not telling his greedy children, he proves that he does not relapse into the old behavior, but rather knows that he can trust the virtues of Beauty.*

150 degrees: Tensions are high and growth is happening quickly. No matter what is being done, whether actions and reactions happen out of trust or fear, they amplify the inner attitude.	
When Beauty set off with her father the two heartless girls rubbed their eyes with an onion, so as to seem tearful; but her brothers wept in reality, as did also the merchant. Beauty alone did not cry, because she did not want to add to their sorrow. The horse took the road to the palace, and by evening they espied it, all lit up as before.	*Beauty's inner attitude is calm, and she seems to feel the connection to the divine. Again, the horse, as a representative of the Moon and her cyclical rhythm, brings them straight to the realm of the goddess. That the Moon and the goddess are tightly connected is also shown with the image of them reaching the castle by evening, where all is lit up (like the Moon).*

The Fourth Segment: Attuning to the Cosmic Order

154.28 degrees: Direct exposure to the mysterious, transcending forces at work. It serves to experience their vast power and become familiar with their laws.	
An empty stable awaited the nag, and when the good merchant and his daughter entered the great hall, they found there a table magnificently laid for two people. The merchant had not the heart to eat, but Beauty, forcing herself to appear calm, sat down and served him.	*An empty stable is waiting for the horse, which is another sign that it was the horse's lunar quality that brought them to the divine realms. It is like coming home for all of them. Beauty and her father are highly welcome.*

160 degrees: Witnessing the divine workings. The potential of a wholesome life is unfolding. The opportunity presents itself to contribute to a more balanced human reality.	
Since the Beast had provided such splendid fare, she thought to herself, he must presumably be anxious to fatten her up before eating her.	*They now get exposed to the generosity and abundance of the divine, and thus get to witness her workings. This is natural and how it should be, however, coming from a society full of greed, they cannot believe this is benevolent. Rather they are wary about it.*

165 degrees (strong lunar influence): Fulfillment draws near.	
When they had finished supper they heard a terrible noise. With tears the merchant bade farewell to his daughter, for he knew it was the Beast. Beauty herself could not help trembling at the awful apparition, but she did her best to compose herself.	*It is the power of the divine energy they encounter now.*

180 degrees: Manifestation and acknowledgement of the new status by the environment. Power is gained or lost again.	
The Beast asked her if she had come of her own free will, and she timidly answered that such was the case. 'You are indeed kind,' said the Beast, 'and I am much obliged to you.	*Beauty somehow seems to be able to recognize and appreciate the goddess's presence. The beast acknowledges her good intentions.*

195 degrees (strong lunar influence): Potential dangers from unresolved shadow forces need to be taken into account.	
'You, my good man, will depart to-morrow morning, and you must not think of coming back again. Good-bye, Beauty!' 'Good-bye, Beast!' she answered. Thereupon the monster suddenly disappeared. 'Daughter,' said the merchant, embracing Beauty, 'I am nearly dead with fright. Let me be the one to stay here!'	*In the face of the divine, it needs to be done what needs to be done. There is a lot of tension. One wrong word or action could jeopardize everything.*

200 degrees: A testing phase now exposes the level of integrity in the human's environment.	
'No, father,' said Beauty, firmly, 'you must go tomorrow morning, and leave me to the mercy of heaven. Perhaps pity will be taken on me.' They retired to rest, thinking they would not sleep at all during the night, but they were hardly in bed before their eyes were closed in sleep. In her dreams there appeared to Beauty a lady, who said to her: 'Your virtuous character pleases me, Beauty. In thus undertaking to give your life to save your father you have performed an act of goodness which shall not go unrewarded.'	*It is the goddess in her appearance as a fairy who speaks to Beauty in her dream. She acknowledges her willingness and personal integrity to fulfill the contract.*

The Fifth Segment: Anchoring the New Reality

205.42 degrees: The extent of the newly gained power becomes evident and is mirrored by increased resistance from the environment.	
...As soon as her father had gone Beauty sat down in the great hall and began to cry. But she had plenty of courage, and after imploring divine protection she determined to grieve no more during the short time she had yet to live. She was convinced that the Beast would devour her that night, but made up her mind that in the interval she would walk about and have a look at this beautiful castle, the splendor of which she could not but admire. Imagine her surprise when she came upon a door on which were the words 'Beauty's Room'! She quickly opened this door, and was dazzled by the magnificence of the appointments within. 'They are evidently anxious that I should not be dull,' she murmured, as she caught sight of a large book-case, a harpsichord, and several volumes of music. A moment later another thought crossed her mind. 'If I had only a day to spend here,' she reflected, 'such provision would surely not have been made for me.' This notion gave her fresh courage. She opened the bookcase, and found a book in which was written, in letters of gold: 'Ask for anything you wish: you are mistress of all here.' 'Alas!' she said with a sigh, 'my only wish is to see my poor father, and to know what he is doing.' As she said this to herself she glanced at a large mirror. Imagine her astonishment when she perceived her home reflected in it, and saw her father just approaching. Sorrow was written	*In this lengthy passage, Beauty learns not to fear the goddess. What in Mother Holle was said in only one or two sentences, is here beautifully described in detail: How the realm of the goddess looks like, which values count, how everybody lives for free here and is nurtured on body, mind and spirit. What counts are sincere values and not flattery.* *So, Beauty is getting to know the goddess as she truly is, maybe frightening, yet also straightforward and benevolent, but whom in her culture has come to be called a beast. Slowly but surely, she is peeling off her layers of preconceived notions by judging from the heart. Thus, she gets to know the divine creative energy, which explicitly lays things into her hands: "It is you who are mistress."*

on his face; but when her sisters came to meet him it was impossible not to detect, despite the grimaces with which they tried to simulate grief, the satisfaction they felt at the loss of their sister. In a moment the vision faded away, yet Beauty could not but think that the Beast was very kind, and that she had nothing much to fear from him. At midday she found the table laid, and during her meal she enjoyed an excellent concert, though the performers were invisible. But in the evening, as she was about to sit down at the table, she heard the noise made by the Beast, and quaked in spite of herself. 'Beauty,' said the monster to her, 'may I watch you have your supper?' 'You are master here,' said the trembling Beauty. 'Not so,' replied the Beast; 'it is you who are mistress; you have only to tell me to go, if my presence annoys you, and I will go immediately. 'Tell me, now, do you not consider me very ugly?' – 'I do,' said Beauty, 'since I must speak the truth; but I think you are also very kind.' 'It is as you say,' said the monster; 'and in addition to being ugly, I lack intelligence. As I am well aware, I am a mere beast.' 'It is not the way with stupid people,' answered Beauty, 'to admit a lack of intelligence. Fools never realize it.' 'Sup well, Beauty,' said the monster, 'and try to banish dullness from your home—for all about you is yours, and I should be sorry to think you were not happy.' 'You are indeed kind,' said Beauty. 'With one thing, I must own, I am well pleased, and that is your kind heart. When I think of that you no longer seem to be ugly.'	*Beauty even finds a way of glancing into the other world, where her father has just come home. This mirror shows her the truth, how her sisters truly are stripped of their masks of fake friendliness. This perspective is offered to her due to her sincerity and her values of integrity.*

'Oh yes,' answered the Beast, 'I have a good heart, right enough, but I am a monster.' 'There are many men,' said Beauty, 'who make worse monsters than you, and I prefer you, notwithstanding your looks, to those who under the semblance of men hide false, corrupt, and ungrateful hearts.' The Beast replied that if only he had a grain of wit he would compliment her in the grand style by way of thanks; but that being so stupid he could only say he was much obliged. Beauty ate with a good appetite, for she now had scarcely any fear of the Beast.	

210 degrees: As the test of integrity comes to a close, the danger of losing identity increases, but holding on to the mission is what offers protection, as well as awareness of what has been learned so far.	
But she nearly died of fright when he put this question to her: 'Beauty, will you be my wife?' For some time she did not answer, fearing lest she might anger the monster by her refusal. She summoned up courage at last to say, rather fearfully, 'No, Beast! '	*It is the same situation as when Golden Mary says to Mother Holle that she wants to go home. If the girl stays in the realm of the goddess, and in Beauty's case, marries the goddess, she will lose her human identity and her physical life. She would get absorbed or devoured and stay in the goddess's realm for good. At one point, she would return in a new body, in a new incarnation, as the Neolithic belief goes. It is a critical moment in all wonder tales. The personal mission must be remembered at this point.*

216 degrees (strong lunar influence): A passage is erected over which a crossing into a new life becomes possible.	
The poor monster gave forth so terrible a sigh that the noise of it went whistling through the whole palace. But to Beauty's speedy relief the Beast sadly took his leave and left the room, turning several times as he did so to look once more at her. Left alone, Beauty was moved by great compassion for this poor Beast. 'What a pity he is so ugly,' she said, 'for he is so good.'	*If Beauty keeps up her firm connection to her physical life and decides to fulfill her mission to make the family's future a better one by collaborating with the goddess, she is given the opportunity to do so now. She will be able to cross over into her world and integrate her newly gained wisdom.*

225 degrees: It is time to firmly anchor the new reality, otherwise the lunar energy vanishes into oblivion again.	
Beauty passed three months… and every day Beauty was made aware of fresh kindnesses on the part of the monster. Through seeing him often she had become accustomed to his ugliness…. One thing alone troubled Beauty; every evening, before retiring to bed, the monster asked her if she would be his wife, and seemed overwhelmed with grief when she refused. One day she said to him: 'You distress me, Beast. I wish I could marry you, but I cannot deceive you by allowing you to believe that that can ever be. I will always be your friend—be content with that.' 'Needs must,' said the Beast. 'But let me make the position plain. I know I am very terrible, but I love you very much, and I shall be very happy if you will only remain here. Promise that you will never leave me.' Beauty blushed at these words. She had seen in her mirror that her father was stricken down by the sorrow of having lost her, and she wished very much to see him again.	*Beauty is still torn between the worlds. However, a human girl cannot marry the goddess. She has sacred functions on the material plane, namely to create physical offspring and act as the goddess's representative. A decision is pending, and things are leading up to a crossroads of destiny.*

230 degrees: A crossroads of destiny shows the road to mastery.

'I would willingly promise to remain with you always,' she said to the Beast, 'but I have so great a desire to see my father again that I shall die of grief if you refuse me this boon.'	*Whatever decision Beauty makes is fine. If she decides to marry the Beast and die to the material world, or whether she goes back to be the surrogate of the goddess, both roads are fine. There is no judgment.*

240 degrees: The vision of mastery inspires a new future.

'I would rather die myself than cause you grief,' said the monster. 'I will send you back to your father. You shall stay with him, and your Beast shall die of sorrow at your departure.' 'No, no,' said Beauty, crying; 'I like you too much to wish to cause your death. I promise you I will return in eight days. You have shown me that my sisters are married, and that my brothers have joined the army. My father is all alone; let me stay with him one week.'	*Beauty must bring back her insights to her own world. She must make a connection between the two worlds and report about the existence of the otherworld and the goddess who lives there. "Do not forget me again!" seems to be the urgent plea of the goddess. She cares of humanities' well-being and wishes for a lasting connection.*

245 degrees: What might seem bad at first presents itself as a chance to turn matters around.	
'You shall be with him to-morrow morning,' said the Beast. 'But remember your promise. All you have to do when you want to return is to put your ring on a table when you are going to bed. Good-bye, Beauty!' As usual, the Beast sighed when he said these last words, and Beauty went to bed quite down-hearted at having grieved him.	*The fact that in her realm everybody is free, and their own master asks the goddess to model this exact principle. She lets Beauty have her own free will and gives her a magical ring, which will bring her back any time. This is the offer for a sacred marriage between the divine and the human. However, the ring also symbolizes the cycles. Here lies the promise of the goddess: A human will always find a way back to the divine realm when attuning to the cosmic cycles.*

252 degrees (strong lunar influence): The connection to the lunar energy has become very strong so that wounds can heal.	
When she woke the next morning she found she was in her father's house. She rang a little bell which stood by the side of her bed, and it was answered by their servant, who gave a great cry at sight of her. The good man came running at the noise, and was overwhelmed with joy at the sight of his dear daughter.... It occurred to Beauty that she had no clothes to put on; but the servant told her that she had just discovered in the next room a chest full of dresses trimmed with gold and studded with diamonds.	*The elixir her father originally received was his dear life and the chance to create a better future for his children by collaborating with the goddess. What Beauty made of this gift became very powerful. She met the goddess in the form of a beast and became aware of her kind heart, despite the fact that her culture referred to the lunar aspect of the divine as a "beast." Such societal wounds can heal now. Now, she sees that this inner-knowing and the inner-connection will equip her with all she ever needs.*

255 degrees: An opportunity like a diamond in the rough presents itself.	
Beauty felt grateful to the Beast for this attention, and having selected the simplest of the gowns she bade the servant pack up the others, as she wished to send them as presents to her sisters. The words were hardly out of her mouth when the chest disappeared.	*The gowns in the chest are intended for Beauty and not her sisters. As modest as she is, she must wear them, they are her "merits" given to her by the goddess. They cannot be handed over. The gift is a promise of a new future.*

The Sixth Segment: Creating a New Future

257.08 degrees: A change of perspective occurs. It is the end of what was before.	
Her father expressed the opinion that the Beast wished her to keep them all for herself, and in a trice dresses and chest were back again where they were before.	*It is more obvious for other people to see and her father recognizes the new quality she brought back from the realm of the goddess. The gowns symbolize the new aura emanating from Beauty. Also, Golden Mary could not hand over the "gold" she had deserved, as it was her "aura."*

270 degrees: Life is experienced from the changed viewpoint, which marks a new beginning.	
When Beauty had dressed she learned that her sisters, with their husbands, had arrived. Both were very unhappy.... The sisters were greatly mortified when they saw Beauty dressed like a princess, and more beautiful than the dawn....	*Beauty now changes perspectives in that she wears her merits for everybody to see. This makes her sisters envious. Beauty will have to grow into her own mastery.*

280 degrees (strong lunar influence): The foundation for a new life is laid.	
. . . 'Sister,' said the elder, 'I have an idea. Let us try to persuade her to stay here longer than the eight days. Her stupid Beast will fly into a rage when he finds she has broken her word, and will very likely devour her.'... When the eight days had passed the two sisters tore their hair, and showed such grief over her departure that she promised to remain another eight days. Beauty reproached herself, nevertheless, with the grief she was causing to the poor Beast; moreover, she greatly missed not seeing him.	*As much as Beauty feels for her sisters, who try to keep her from her inner connection to the goddess and the lunar energy, having experienced the Beast's purity of heart, Beauty will always remain connected to the goddess. There is still her longing for completeness and a higher consciousness. It secretly guides and pulls her to mastery.*

285 degrees: The divine creative energies can be tapped into to create a new life.	
On the tenth night of her stay in her father's house she dreamed that she was in the palace garden, where she saw the Beast lying on the grass nearly dead, and that he upbraided her for her ingratitude. Beauty woke up with a start, and burst into tears.	*The connection is still strong, even if Beauty does not consciously think about it all the time. If needed, the information and connection wells up from the unconscious.*

288 degrees: A legacy is created.	
'I am indeed very wicked,' she said, 'to cause so much grief to a Beast who has shown me nothing but kindness. Is it his fault that he is so ugly, and has so few wits? He is good, and that makes up for all the rest. Why did I not wish to marry him? I should have been a good deal happier with him than my sisters are with their husbands. It is neither good looks nor brains in a husband that make a woman happy; it is beauty of character, virtue, kindness'.	*Since Beauty has returned to her own world, she can now safely consider "marrying" the beast/goddess. Beauty is thus welcoming the cosmic energy, the goddess, in all her shades. With it, she starts to create a lasting change. She will be the first woman in her family to do things differently, in alignment with the cosmic order. It is her chance to leave a legacy for future generations.*

300 degrees: What once was only a vision can now become a living reality.	
'All these qualities the Beast has. I admit I have no love for him, but he has my esteem, friendship, and gratitude. At all events I must not make him miserable, or I shall reproach myself all my life.'	*For Beauty it is still a stretch to "love" the mother goddess which has been sold to her by her culture as being "the beast," however she starts to appreciate the divine for her integral qualities. And this is the bridge between humanity and the divine realm.*

305 degrees (strong lunar influence): The power of the alignment keeps inspiring you.	
With these words Beauty rose and placed her ring on the table.	*Placing the ring on the table means that she agrees to this new approach to life and to live in sync with the cycles of the Sun and the Moon, the balanced calendar. With it she acknowledges their equal "marriage."*

The Seventh Segment: Reaching Mastery

308.34 degrees: Mastery is reached.	
Hardly had she returned to her bed than she was asleep, and when she woke the next morning she saw with joy that she was in the Beast's palace.	*The connection is strong and the attunement to the cycles easy. Beauty masterfully moves between both worlds and makes the right choices that are aligned with the cosmic order.*

315 degrees: Wise leadership exists at the highest level.	
She dressed in her very best on purpose to please him, and nearly died of impatience all day.... but no Beast appeared. Beauty now thought she must have caused his death, and rushed about the palace with loud despairing cries.	*Beauty cannot just wait around, being passive when partnering with the goddess. She needs to display wise leadership. What needs to be done next?*

320 degrees: Time of harvest and letting go of the work.	
She looked everywhere, and at last, recalling her dream, dashed into the garden by the canal, where she had seen him in her sleep. There she found the poor Beast lying unconscious, and thought he must be dead.	*She recalls her dream, which at the time held the promise "that the divine creative energies can be tapped into." Thanks to that dream, she finds the Beast again. The potential of her higher purpose (higher consciousness and completeness of self) is now unfolding its powerful energy, ready to transform and heal the world.*

324 degrees: A new and different future is triggered.	
She threw herself on his body, all her horror of his looks forgotten, and, feeling his heart still beat, fetched water from the canal and threw it on his face.	*There is love for the cosmic "beast" after all. Water is the Moon's element, and by fetching it and throwing it on his face, she demonstrates that she knows.*

330 degrees: What was initially missing is now fully present.	
The Beast opened his eyes and said to Beauty: 'You forgot your promise. The grief I felt at having lost you made me resolve to die of hunger; but I die content since I have the pleasure of seeing you once more.' 'Dear Beast, you shall not die,' said Beauty; 'you shall live and become my husband. Here and now I offer you my hand, and swear that I will marry none but you. Alas, I fancied I felt only friendship for you, but the sorrow I have experienced clearly proves to me that I cannot live without you.'	*There is a little bit of French stage drama here, however, it is the moment Beauty fully acknowledges the lunar quality and says yes to it. The missing quality, which had been missing at 30 degrees is now fully recovered in Beauty's life. Back then, the two sisters demonstrated that they were lacking rhythm and caring, but instead lived their lives without structure and only focused on themselves. The gesture of fetching water is a gesture of empathy, of knowing what the other needs, but also a demonstration that she now understands the rhythmical lunar quality of water, which is what the divine/beast needs in order to live (for humans). With this action, Beauty displays her mastery in dealing with the divine.*

334.38 degrees (strong lunar influence): Everything falls into the right place, just as it should be.	
Beauty had scarcely uttered these words when the castle became ablaze with lights before her eyes: fireworks, music—all proclaimed a feast. But these splendors were lost on her: she turned to her dear Beast, still trembling for his danger. Judge of her surprise now! At her feet she saw no longer the Beast, who had disappeared, but a prince, more beautiful than Love himself, who thanked her for having put an end to his enchantment.	*Now she has reached mastery. This transforms everything. Yet, she does not stand in awe of herself, but rather puts her focus on the Beast, who no longer is a monster but a prince! The goddess sent her a partner worthy of her. The enchantment, originally caused by a society that suppressed the lunar energy, is solved. The lunar energies will now be at everybody's disposal as the couple becomes leaders, a queen and her king.*

In the French version, there is a lengthy moral embellishment at this point in the story, which I cut out to follow the aspect build-up.[65]

342 degrees: Stepping back through destiny's gate.	
In a trice, with a tap of her hand, the fairy transported them all to the prince's realm,	*The goddess appears again in her fairy aspect, bringing them back to their regular life, where they will model a complete and balanced way of life for all to see, a life that no longer excludes the wisdom of nature and her cycles. The prerequisites for a healthy renewal of their society is therefore given.*

347.14 degrees: All divine creative energies are honored.	
where his subjects were delighted to see him again.	*The formerly missing lunar quality is back, for all to see. Balance and the connection to the divine is restored. All are invited to partake in the abundance this completeness brings.*

65 "*With good reason were her eyes riveted upon the prince, but she asked him nevertheless where the Beast had gone. 'You see him at your feet,' answered the prince. 'A wicked fairy condemned me to retain that form until some beautiful girl should consent to marry me, and she forbade me to betray any sign of intelligence. You alone in all the world could show yourself susceptible to the kindness of my character, and in offering you my crown I do but discharge the obligation that I owe you.'*
In agreeable surprise Beauty offered her hand to the handsome prince, and assisted him to rise. Together they repaired to the castle, and Beauty was overcome with joy to find, assembled in the hall, her father and her entire family. The lady who had appeared to her in her dream had had them transported to the castle.
'Beauty,' said this lady (who was a celebrated fairy), 'come and receive the reward of your noble choice. You preferred merit to either beauty or wit, and you certainly deserve to find these qualities combined in one person. It is your destiny to become a great queen, but I hope that the pomp of royalty will not destroy your virtues. As for you, ladies,' she continued, turning to Beauty's two sisters, 'I know your hearts and the malice they harbour. Your doom is to become statues, and under the stone that wraps you round to retain all your feelings. You will stand at the door of your sister's palace, and I can visit no greater punishment upon you than that you shall be witnesses of her happiness. Only when you recognise your faults can you return to your present shape, and I am very much afraid that you will be statues for ever. Pride, ill-temper, 'Your doom is to become statues' greed, and laziness can all be corrected, but nothing short of a miracle will turn a wicked and envious heart.'"

354 degrees: The new is already calling.	
He married Beauty, and they lived together for a long time in happiness the more perfect because it was founded on virtue.	*Happiness and balance are now restored, because they are founded on the virtues of integrity. Integrity means accounting for all the divine creative energies, the lunar as well as the solar ones.*

The concept of a woman becoming a surrogate of the goddess, as described in Chapter 11, is very clearly illustrated here. But there is also the message that *the divine can only be collaborated with, when its lunar, feminine aspect is welcomed, and the natural cycles are considered.* The entire tale is directed toward that big moment of transformation at the end, the moment of Beauty's saying *yes* to the Beast alias the goddess. In that very moment, the goddess provides her with a prince, a real man in the physical world, whom she can marry and have children with. Everything else would make no sense. Beauty representing a real human being with a real physical life needs a real physical partner to have children with, this is how she will be of service to the divine on the physical plane.

Acknowledgments

The writing of this book was a long process. People around me truly needed a long breath to keep up with my theories, down times, triumphs, questions, doubts, getting enraged about patriarchy, and being inspired by new insights. I repeatedly exclaimed "Now, I know what my book is about!" all the while cracking up at how insane this sounded. How could I express in words what I hardly knew myself? All I knew was that I was not going to give up until I would find answers that made sense. The true extent of the matter only revealed itself to me in the very end. So, thank you, my dear family Hansjürg, Felicia, and Elea, and thank you my dear friends, Sascha Beer, Andrea Bitterlin, Fabienne Burri, Ursula and Viola Graf, Barbara Martig, Betina Trunsperger, and Amanda Williams for not declaring me crazy, but rather that you kept asking me about my progress and the latest findings.

You, my dearest Hansjürg were the most supportive husband there can be. From the bottom of my heart I thank you that you were open to discuss my ideas anytime and that you always critically questioned them. Thank you for your relentless support, reading and double checking my statements and chapters until the very last moment.

I couldn't have written this book if it weren't for you, my wonderful and smart daughters. Felicia, at the time of my writing, you were studying anthropology and religion at the University of Fribourg. You supported me for hours on end by sharing your know-how and source books, reading chapter after chapter and giving me valuable feedback. You played a vital part in shaping this book into what it is. And you, my younger daughter, Elea, shared the world of fairy tales with me from an early age. You accompanied me into its magic realm and together we explored the forests, the museums, and the archeological sites near our house and abroad. You listened patiently to all my theories, questioned them as you grew older, and added your keen observations. I am so proud of what supportive daughters I have in you. Thank you from the bottom of my heart.

If it weren't for you, my dear friends at the Land of Legends in Ljungby, Sweden, I would not have been able to leave my set viewpoints on interpreting folklore. Dörthe Drewsen, your way of conveying the oral heritage and its historical background shifted my entire perception of the folk tales. No longer did I interpret them only psychologically, but I started to see them as coming straight out of life, a life of people with other belief systems. Thank you so much for patiently answering all my questions and letting me see the tales through the eyes of folk who lived so close to nature that they still witnessed its magic in everyday life.

At the same time, I am ever so grateful to you, Meg Nömgård, head of the Land of Legends, the "Sagomuseet" in Ljungby, for always welcoming me with open arms, entrusting me with telling stories and spending time in this magical place. For me, the museum is a window to a long-lost world, but also an incredibly valuable treasure chest for my research.

Thank you, Robin Heath, for your encouragement and your truly inspiring archeo-astronomical studies and the very detailed books you wrote on it. If it weren't for you, I would have never been able to answer that one last question: How on earth did the Neolithic people know about the lunar nodes? Your books and lectures deepened my understanding of the Neolithic worldview as it is displayed in wonder tales.

I also would like to pay tribute to the many professionals who supported me in publishing this book: my former mentor, Tina Uhlmann, who encouraged me to write this book in the first place, and my editors Judith Steinemann, Kendall Davies, Katie McCandless and Beth Hammock. You patiently edited my English and helped me get across what I wanted to say in a language that wasn't my mother tongue. Judy, you had to put up with me in the beginning of the manuscript, when I hardly knew myself where the research was going to take me. Thank you for bearing with me and always supporting and encouraging me. Kendall, you gave me valuable feedback from an outsider's standpoint, Katie, you came in when I needed a sharp eye on the last and very complex third part and Beth, you carefully smoothed out and polished the end product. Thank you all very much. Thank you, Jack and Cathy Davis from Davis Creative, for the beautiful cover and interior design as well as for your support in bringing this book into its final shape.

Finally, I am deeply grateful to all my interview partners who filled in my questionnaire regarding their personal hero's journey. The insights I gained from your answers were tremendously helpful and of great importance for this book. Thank you, my dear friend Barbara Martig, for going through your seventy-six years of memories and diaries to see if my theory could withstand the proof of reality. I admire your rich life as a gifted artist, an internationally renowned opera singer, and mother of two. What a wonderful example of a person, a heroine on a journey, who stayed true to her heart and turned into a wise elder along the road. I am happy and honored to be your friend.

References of Used Folklore

“The Truth and Folk Tale”: „Neue jüdische Märchen“, Fischer, 1986

“Mother Hulda blesses the Earth”: “Volksagen und Märchen um Frau Holle”, Karl Paetow, Adolf Sponholtz Verlag, 1962, arranged by Djamila Jaenike, translated by Andrea Hofman

“The Greedy Farmer”: “Innerschweizerische Sagen und Legenden“, Anna Ithen, SAVK Band 2, 1898, translated by Andrea Hofman

“The Pumpkin Birth”: “Sagen und Märchen aus dem Oberwallis“, Jegerlehner u. Bächtold-Stäubli, 1913, translated by Andrea Hofman

“Michel and Nérine”: “Märchen und Sagen der Schweiz“, Hans Peter Treichler, Silva-Verlag, Orell Füssli, 1989, translated by Andrea Hofman

“The Glass Fountain”: “Kinder- und Hausmärchen aus der Schweiz“, Otto Sutermeister, Aarau: H.R. Sauerländer, 1869, translated by Andrea Hofman

“The Three Wishes”: “More English Fairy Tales”, Joseph Jacobs, 1894

“The Legend of the Loom”: “Von Lebertran bis Totemtier“, NONAM Skript, Publikation, 2011, translated by Andrea Hofman

“Mother Holle”: “Grimm’s Household Tales” translated by Margaret Hunt, 1884

“Beauty and The Beast”: “Old-Time Stories” (Charles Perrault), Jeanne-Marie Le Prince de Beaumont, translated by A. E. Johnson, 1921

About the Author

Andrea Hofman is a researcher of folklore, storyteller and astrologer. From a very young age, she was intrigued by the magical world of fairy tales. In her favorite childhood tale, the heroine asks the Sun, Moon, and stars for advice—and funnily enough, that is exactly what Andrea ended up doing when she grew up! Andrea studied astrology and became fascinated with the stories that had been written by life itself. At one point in her studies, she compared fairy tales to real-life biographies and found that they shared the same rhythm. Fascinated, she began to conduct more research and wrote down her observations, not even dreaming that she was about to find the key to an ancient cosmic wisdom.

Andrea lives in the German part of Switzerland. She lectures, writes, tells stories, and frequently travels to Sweden (to collaborate with the Land of Legends), the United Kingdom, and many other destinations, where she tries to find remnants of the ancestral wisdom. To learn more about Andrea and her work, visit her website at www.andreahofman.com.

Index

A

B

C

D

E

F

G

H

I

J

K

L

M

Q

R

S

T

U

V

W

Z

37223093R00195

Printed in Poland
by Amazon Fulfillment
Poland Sp. z o.o., Wrocław